GOD'S WILL

FOR YOUR LIFE

GOD'S WILL
FOR YOUR LIFE

A practical study of the scriptural principles involved in determining and doing the will of God in daily Christian living

BY
S. MAXWELL CODER

MOODY PRESS
CHICAGO

Moody Press, a ministry of the Moody Bible Institute, is
designed for education, evangelization and edification.
If we may assist you in knowing more about Christ and
the Christian life, please write us without obligation to:
Moody Press, c/o MLM, Chicago, Illinois 60610.

ISBN: 0-8024-3055-4

Printed in the United States of America

CONTENTS

1

GOD HAS A PLAN FOR EVERY LIFE

ONE OF THE MOST PRACTICAL and inspiring subjects to be found in the Bible is the revelation that God has a plan for every life. When that plan is discovered and followed, it brings greater happiness and success than could be achieved in any other conceivable set of circumstances. This teaching of the Scriptures has an especially strong appeal to Christian young people with life still before them.

The world knows nothing of the concept of a God-planned life, and for some reason many believers have failed to realize how much of the Bible is devoted to it. As a result, one constantly meets people who have missed the way somewhere. They made wrong choices, overlooked golden opportunities, and finally resigned themselves to a life of unpleasant drudgery or disappointed hopes. Although they would give almost anything to be able to make a fresh start, they know of no way to rectify the mistake of having planned their own lives and failed.

No instructed Christian needs to fear any such unhappy prospect. God has made us, and He knows our capacities, our weaknesses, our innermost longings and aspirations. There is a divine blueprint for each one of God's people. It is exactly suited to our own peculiar needs, so that it enables us to make the most of our possibilities. It has not only this life in view, but also the life to come. It is easy to discover what it is. In fact, the Lord is more desirous that we learn His plan than we ourselves are. He has made every provision to enable us to follow it. If we have not previously sought to live in accordance with it, we can begin at once, no matter what our age.

This is a neglected truth of the Scriptures, but a prominent one. It is of great importance; it is exceedingly precious to the soul. To take but one detail from the riches of truth dealing with the subject, God promises to give us the desires of our hearts if we meet the simple conditions set forth in the Word (Ps. 37:4). Who can remain indifferent in the face of a guarantee like this, backed as it is by the faithfulness of God?

This is Reasonable

According to reason, God has a plan for every Christian. Whatever we do, whether we are building a model, or making a dress, or playing a game, our minds demand that we have a plan to follow. We turn quite naturally to a timetable or a road map when we are about to travel to a distant point.

Everywhere we look in the universe around us, we find intelligent planning. A snowflake or a flower viewed through a microscope shows unmistakable evidence of wonderful design. Our telescopes reveal such a careful arrangement of the movement of the heavenly bodies that we set our watches by them. Every mineral has a purpose. Plants have specific functions to perform, in purifying and perfuming the air, providing food for men and animals, beautifying the earth during life, and enriching the soil in death.

When we reflect that we are the highest of God's earthly creatures, destined for a place in the future even above that of the angels, we are forced to the conclusion that God must have a special work for us to do during our time on earth. He has made us; every talent we possess has come from Him; He has purchased us at the awful cost of the blood of His Son. It is unthinkable that He should intend us to live in uncertainty and confusion, with no worthwhile goal to achieve. We are the special objects of His love. We were upon His heart before the world was created (Eph. 1:4). If He guides the moon, though it is dead and cold, He will surely guide us in such a way as to satisfy every longing He has implanted within us. It is reasonable to believe that we are no exception to the law of creation. God has a purpose for everything in His universe.

This Is Practical

According to experience, there is a divine plan for each believer. Multitudes of God's people have found His plan for their lives and followed it. For Abraham it meant leaving the city of Ur of the Chaldees and spending the remainder of his years in tents (Heb. 11:8-10). For Moses it meant giving up the wealth and honor he had enjoyed in Egypt, to begin a life of wandering in the wilderness (Heb. 11:24-27). For David it meant leaving the sheepfold where he had spent his boyhood, and sitting on the throne of Israel (I Chron. 17:7).

Christian literature furnishes many examples of men and women who dedicated their lives to doing God's will, in every kind of occupation. Whether their work was quite commonplace and obscure, or so unusual as to make them outstanding, they steadfastly walked with God.

Among the more prominent of these may be mentioned Sir Robert Anderson, famous head of Scotland Yard and author of popular books of Bible study. In the business world, the name of Henry P. Crowell stands out as a convincing illustration of what God can do through a man who honors Him. Many cities have Christian businessmen's groups made up of others of like faith. Great lawyers like Simon Greenleaf and great statesmen like William E. Gladstone are known to history for their zeal in the defense of the faith. Dr. Howard A. Kelly, of Johns Hopkins University, a world-renowned surgeon, was also a noted evangelical believer who sought always to follow Christ. Outstanding scientists like Newton, Faraday, Pasteur and Fleming tried with all humility to do the Lord's will for them.

Monica, mother of St. Augustine, is an example of those women who have believed God's will was to raise children for His glory. Mary Slessor, on the other hand, felt called to leave the factory for the mission field, just as William Carey left the cobbler's bench and C. T. Studd the university classroom. These few names are representative of a host of others who consciously sought to conform their lives to the divine program.

This Is Scriptural

According to revelation, God has a plan for each of us. The Bible teaching about the subject is vast. Earthly parents may direct the education of their children into paths leading to a lifework which seems desirable, but only God has the infinite wisdom and knowledge needed to guide an individual into the work for which he was endowed at birth. The Lord may, of course, use the prayerful efforts of godly parents to guard their children from mistakes in the choice of a vocation. He also uses our natural inclinations, our environment, and the circumstances which come to us.

Little Is Much with God

The personal interest God shows in each one of us, as it is revealed in the Word, is astonishing. It should lead us to expect to find a rich body of truth about the pathway in which He wants us to walk. The very hairs of our heads are numbered (Matt. 10:30). The Lord knows our sorrows (Exod. 3:7); He records our tears (Ps. 56:8). He takes note of our downsittings and our uprisings (Ps. 139:2). All our thoughts, our ways and our words are known to Him (Ps. 139:2-6). A book of remembrance is written before Him for those who fear the Lord and think upon His name (Mal. 3:16).

A number of facts about God's program appears from a study of the many passages dealing with it which are scattered throughout the Scriptures. The Old and New Testaments are in perfect agreement; each provides a wealth of truth about the divine plan.

1. It Is a Personal Program

Every believer has the right to take the words of Psalm 32:8 as though they were written just for him. "I will instruct thee and teach thee in the way which thou shalt go: I will guide thee with mine eye." An individual pathway is in view, as distinguished from the general way of righteousness set before all Christians. Three words are used to tell us how the Lord makes known to us the way in which we are to go.

Each word is full of meaning in the Hebrew tongue used by the psalmist. "Instruction" is the enlightening of the intelligence. "Teaching" is the pointing out of a definite course. "Guidance" is the advice needed for particular problems. And notice that God undertakes to do all three for us; He says, "I will."

The fact that we have a part to play in making His will our will is evident from the following verse, which contains a warning that He may enforce our obedience if necessary, exactly as we use a bit and bridle to compel a beast of burden to go where we want it to go. A parallel thought occurs in Acts 9:5: "It is hard for thee to kick against the pricks." The Lord used pricks, or goads, to bring Paul into subjection to Himself. It is the word for an ox goad, used to keep oxen subject to their owner's will.

2. God's Plan Is for Believers Only

When we read all of Psalm 32, we find the promise of guidance is given only to those whose transgressions are forgiven, whose sins are under the blood, who have made confession to God. No unsaved person has any claim to the promises about a divinely planned life. Instead, the ungodly may be used to show forth God's wrath against sin (Rom. 9:22), or, like Nebuchadnezzar, to accomplish the divine purpose in spite of unbelief (Jer. 25:9, 12).

The cloud which directed the people of Israel in their way brought nothing but confusion to the Egyptians (Exod. 14:19, 20). Before anyone may expect to be led through the wilderness of this world by the modern counterpart of the pillar of fire, he must be sure he is numbered among those to whom the promise is addressed. "What man is he that feareth the Lord? him shall he teach in the way that he shall choose" (Ps. 25:12).

3. God's Plan Is Wonderfully Detailed

Incredible as such a revelation may seem at first thought, every step we take is "ordered by the Lord" (Ps. 37:23). He does not always reveal the distant future to us, but He does lead each step of the way. Perhaps several paths lie ahead, each one open and inviting, but we need not fear that we shall make a mistake, for it is written, "He shall direct thy paths" (Prov. 3:6). Paul once found himself in a place where he was for a time uncertain about what he should do. When he tried to enter Asia and Bithynia, the Holy Spirit prevented him, and directed him instead to Philippi in Europe (Acts 16:6-10).

What about the multitude of details making up every life? Can God have a purpose in each one? His Word so declares in unmistakable terms: "And we know that all things work together for good to them that love God, to them who are the called according to his purpose" (Rom. 8:28). Furthermore, this verse states that *we know* this is true.

4. God's Program Is Continuous

"The Lord shall guide thee continually" (Isa. 58:11). His compassions are new every morning. Once He has undertaken to save us, He will never leave nor forsake us (Heb. 13:5). It does not matter whether we are just beginning the Christian life, or whether we have long known the Lord, He will guide us every moment if we permit Him to do so. He is with us even when we walk through the valley of the shadow (Ps. 23:4).

5. God's Program Is Definite and Specific

"Thine ears shall hear a word behind thee, saying, This is the way, walk ye in it, when ye turn to the right hand, and when ye turn to the left" (Isa. 30:21). We may not hear an audible voice today, but it is still true that "the way of the righteous is made plain" (Prov. 15:19). What is true of the way of salvation is also true of the divine plan: "The wayfaring men, though fools, shall not err therein" (Isa. 35:8).

6. God's Plan Allows for Special Counsel and Wisdom

When doubts come as to exactly what we ought to do, we have the privilege of praying for specific directions: "Cause me to know the way wherein I should walk; for I lift up my soul unto thee" (Ps. 143:8; cf. Ps. 27:11).

When we are confronted with particular problems requiring unusual wisdom, the promise of James 1:5 may acquire a new, wonderful meaning; our daily communion with the Lord will partake of the nature of an important personal consultation. "If any of you lack wisdom, let him ask of God, that giveth to all men liberally, and upbraideth not; and it shall be given him." The only condition is the realization of our own lack! Whether we are facing an important crisis, or simply doing our tasks, we may say with full confidence, "Thou shalt guide me with thy counsel" (Ps. 73:24).

7. God's Plan Is Sure to Be Profitable

From the standpoint of present and future advantages alone, the God-planned life is the only wise course to follow. For honoring the Word of God, Joshua was given the guarantee, "Then thou shalt make thy way prosperous, and then thou shalt have good success" (Josh. 1:8). We have the same promise in Psalm 1:3, "Whatsoever he doeth shall prosper."

With so many about us who have failed in what they sought to do, it is wonderful to know that no Christian need fail to accomplish everything God gives him to do, even during hard times (Jer. 17:7, 8). Not only shall we have prosperity and good success, but we shall have light upon our path (John 8:12), joy in our labors (Acts 20:24), peace in every circumstance (Isa. 26:3; Phil. 4:7), and such satisfaction as cannot be found elsewhere (Ps. 63: 5, 8).

8. The Will of God Is Always Good

Ignorance of the Bible may lead some folk to speak of God's will as though it were an unavoidable evil, to be dreaded and feared. The Word itself, on the other hand, speaks of "that good, and acceptable, and perfect, will of God" (Rom. 12:2). Anyone may prove, or demonstrate, the truth of this by presenting his body to the Lord as a living sacrifice.

9. Doing God's Will Brings Assurance

"If any man willeth to do his will, he shall know of the teaching, whether it is of God" (John 7:17, A.S.V.). This is a Bible truth which may be applied to the knowledge of what God would have us do with our lives, as well as to the knowledge of salvation on receiving Christ (John 6:40). It may be looked upon as a challenge to every Christian to put these things to the test.

One reason some believers lack assurance about their relationship to God is that they have been doing their own will, rather than the will of God. He has put this teaching on the basis of experimental proof, just as we can check a law of physics or chemistry in the laboratory. If we do what He wants us to do, we shall know whether His Word, His program for us individually, is really of God. Nothing could be fairer than this, nor more likely to appeal to the minds of young people in modern times. "These things have I written unto you that believe on the name of the Son of God; that ye may know" (I John 5:13).

2

WHY IT IS IMPORTANT TO KNOW GOD'S PLAN

AT LEAST SEVEN FACTS are set forth in the Scriptures showing the importance of learning the plan of God for our lives. They may be applied not only to the specific program of God for each individual, but also to the general will of God for all His children, which is a life of constant obedience to His Word. Each of these seven considerations is sufficient in itself to make it imperative that we seriously face the question of what the Lord would have us do.

1. We are Incapable of Planning Our Own Lives

"O Lord, I know that the way of man is not in himself: it is not in man that walketh to direct his steps" (Jer. 10:23). We lack the capacity to guide our steps aright. Sin has deprived mankind of its steering mechanism. It might be more accurate to say that sin has deprived man of that living contact with God by which He communicates His perfect will to His creatures.

We are sure to go astray unless we learn and follow God's will. "All we like sheep have gone astray; we have turned every one to his own way" (Isa. 53:6). Such a statement permits of no exceptions; our way is always wrong. The writer of Psalm 119:176, godly as he was, did not hesitate to say to the Lord, "I have gone astray like a lost sheep; seek thy servant; for I do not forget thy commandments."

It is because of what the Lord Jesus did for us on Calvary that our lost communion with God has been restored. When we pray. "Thy will be done in earth, as it is in heaven" (Matt. 6:10), we are seeking to conform our lives to God's plan, and we are likewise looking forward to the time when the full results of the cross will be seen on earth, as the prayer, "Thy kingdom come," is answered.

2. Only God Knows the Future

"I am God, and there is none like me, declaring the end from the beginning, and from ancient times the things that are not yet done" (Isa. 46:9, 10). We do not know what lies ahead, but God does, and we have His reassuring promise, "I am the Lord thy God which teacheth thee to profit, which leadeth thee by the way that thou shouldest go" (Isa. 48:17). If we fail to heed His voice, His sorrowful tones echo in our hearts, "O that thou hadst hearkened to my commandments! then had thy peace been as a river" (v. 18).

Frequently the Scriptures remind us that our future is known to God, "The Lord knoweth the way of the righteous" (Ps. 1:6). In the midst of affliction, Job could say, "He knoweth the way that I take" (Job 23:10). When David was alone among his enemies and hiding in a cave for safety, he knew the Lord had not forsaken him, and he wrote, "When my spirit was overwhelmed within me, then thou knewest my path" (Ps. 142:3).

We know not what a day may bring forth (Prov. 27:1),

but when we dare to believe, as did Samuel, that God's way is perfect, and trust Him to reveal it to us, we may be sure He will make our way perfect, as He did that of the prophet (II Sam. 22:32, 33). Our pathway will be "as the shining light, that shineth more and more unto the perfect day" (Prov. 4:18).

Dark days and uncertainty may sometimes be our experience, but this is anticipated and provided for. "Who is among you that feareth the Lord, that obeyeth the voice of his servant, that walketh in darkness, and hath no light? let him trust in the name of the Lord, and stay upon his God" (Isa. 50:10).

3. The Will of God Brings Lifelong Blessings

Some of these have been mentioned as characteristics of the God-planned life. We shall prosper in the work we undertake, and succeed where others fail. Light, joy, peace and satisfaction will be ours. We shall be made wiser than our enemies, and be given understanding beyond that of our teachers, even beyond that of the ancients (Ps. 119:98-100). No fears about the future will cause alarm.

The knowledge of God's will brings new assurance into our prayer life. "This is the confidence that we have in him, that, if we ask anything according to his will, he heareth us: and if we know that he hear us, whatsoever we ask, we know that we have the petitions we desired of him" (I John 5:14, 15). It would not be easy to find a more blessed promise, nor a greater incentive to learn what it means to pray "according to his will." Obviously, it means our prayers must be in accord with the Word. If a Christian girl insists on marrying an unsaved boy in disregard of God's warning about the unequal yoke (II Cor. 6:14), she cannot expect God to answer her petitions for happiness. The boy who does not honor his father and mother has no right to look for God's blessing on his daily work (Eph. 6:2, 3).

4. The Will of God Brings Blessings in the Life to Come

"The world passeth away, and the lust thereof: but he that doeth the will of God abideth forever" (I John 2:17). This was the life text of D. L. Moody, and the whole world knows the results of his effort to conform his life to it, after he heard the soul-stirring words of his friend Henry Varley, a Christian businessman: "The world has yet to see what God can do with, and for, and through, and in a man who is fully and wholly yielded to Him." Mr. Moody abides forever in glory, and his work abides on earth (John 15:16).

Moses lived with the eternal riches in view, which he knew awaited him for obeying God's will. "He had respect unto the recompense of the reward" (Heb. 11:26). Abraham, Isaac and Jacob endured privation as strangers and pilgrims on the earth, for they "looked for a city which hath foundations, whose builder and maker is God" (Heb. 11:8-16). Christ exhorted, "Lay up for yourselves treasures in heaven" (Matt. 6:20; 19:21).

The apostle Paul spoke of the rigorous discipline demanded of those who seek to win an athletic contest; then pointed out how we too must bring our bodies into subjection, if we are to win the highest prize in the heavenly race (I Cor. 9:24-27). Just before his death, he wrote, "I have fought a good fight, I have finished my course, I have kept the faith: henceforth there is laid up for me a crown of righteousness, which the Lord, the righteous judge, shall give me at that day: and not to me only, but unto all them also that love his appearing" (II Tim. 4:7, 8).

5. God Wants Us to Know His Will

This is evident from the apostolic prayer of Colossians 1:9, "We . . . do not cease to pray for you, and to desire that ye might be filled with the knowledge of his will in all wisdom and spiritual understanding." Near the close of the same epistle is found a further example of God's interest in our learning of His will, as revealed in His servant Epaphras, who is described as "always laboring fervently for you in prayers, that ye may stand perfect and complete in all the will of God" (Col. 4:12).

The abundant provision God has made for us to discover His purpose for us is an indication of how much He desires it. We would conclude that *prayer* is a part of this provision, from the teaching in Colossians, and there are other similar references, as in Psalm 27:11: "Teach me thy way, O Lord, and lead me in a plain path, because of mine enemies."

The Bible is likewise a part of the appointed means to this end. "Thy word is a lamp unto my feet, and a light unto my path" (Ps. 119:105). It has power to keep us from turning aside from the right way, and to restore us if we have turned aside (Ps. 119:1, 9). When the Word is in our hearts, every step we take is sure and safe (Ps. 37:31), so that we are able to say, "I delight to do thy will, O my God: yea, thy law is within my heart" (Ps. 40:8).

The Lord's sovereign control over every *circumstance* of our lives is a third important factor in His making known His program to us. When Joseph was carried into Egypt, his brethren intended it for evil, but God meant it for good (Gen. 50:20). Saul went forth looking for his father's beasts, but he found a kingdom instead (I Sam. 9 and 10). We may rest assured that the Lord will not permit us to remain long in ignorance of what He wants us to do with our lives, if we are willing to follow Him.

6. God Commands Us to Know His Will

"Wherefore be ye not unwise, but understanding what the will of the Lord is" (Eph. 5:17). This is just as much a command as, "Love one another"; or, "Be ye holy"; or, "Pray without ceasing," or any other plain statement of Scripture.

It is easier to understand how we are supposed to begin obeying Ephesians 5:17, if we read the preceding verses. In verse 14 there is a picture of Christians who are asleep to their privileges and responsibilities. Let us suppose this has been our own condition. We must wake up and rise to our feet, for we have new life in Christ. We should be giving evidence that we are truly alive in Him, unlike those around us who are dead in trespasses and sins (Eph. 2:1).

When we have done our part, by separating ourselves from the spiritually dead folks around us, Christ promises to begin to do things for us. Once we are awake and standing true for Him, the word to us is, "Christ shall give thee light." We discern a pathway ahead which His light reveals. The next message is, "See then that ye walk circumspectly, not as fools, but as wise" (Eph. 5:15). "He that is wise winneth souls" (Prov. 11:30, R.V.).

A further word is given, "Redeeming the time, because the days are evil" (Eph. 5:16). This means we are to make good use of our time, devoting it to Christ, remembering that we are always His representatives, whatever we do. Then, having done these necessary things, we shall be able to understand the will of the Lord (v. 17). We shall also be in a position to obey the command, "Be filled with the Spirit" (v. 18).

Since we are required to understand the will of the Lord for us, it is obvious that this is an individual, personal matter for each of us. The Lord may want one person to work in a business office, and another to go to the mission field. He may lead one boy to the farm, and his brother to the United States Senate. One girl will be guided to take up nursing, while her sister will remain all her life in a factory, yet fulfill God's plans as His witness in that place.

More girls are called to be housewives than missionaries. The rearing of children for the glory of the Lord is as noble and important a Christian work as any other. Doubtless the mother of the Wesleys did more for the gospel by bringing up her children in the nurture and admonition of the Lord, than she could have done as a "Christian worker" in the usual sense of the term.

God lays His hand upon more boys to make of them Christian businessmen or tradesmen than pastors and evangelists. It must be remembered that yielding ourselves to God does not mean agreeing to go to Africa, or entering what is usually called "full-time Christian service," or any other particular kind of work. It does mean offering ourselves to God for whatever life plan He may have chosen for us, even if this requires, as it often does, that we remain right where we are, in the place to which He has already brought us, to be His faithful ambassadors in some obscure corner.

7. God Commands Us to Obey His Will

"As the servants of Christ, doing the will of God from the heart" (Eph. 6:6). This is a commandment which ought to send us to prayer and to the study of the Bible to learn His will. "To obey is better than sacrifice, and to hearken than the fat of rams" (I Sam. 15:22). "We ought to obey God rather than men" (Acts 5:29).

There is a general program to be carried out by all good soldiers of Jesus Christ, and there is also a special program for each one. The Lord has designated the objectives to be achieved by all the armies of heaven, but He has also given specific objectives to each one serving in His ranks. If we are trying to follow only the general orders given to everybody who knows Christ, we have missed the fullness of the meaning of Ephesians 6:6, and scores of other passages.

As true believers, we will not neglect any of the Bible precepts governing the Christian life. The grace of God teaches us that, "denying ungodliness and worldly lusts, we should live soberly, righteously, and godly, in this present world; looking for that blessed hope, and the glorious appearing of the great God and our Saviour Jesus Christ" (Titus 2:12, 13). But we also want to do the particular job the Lord has assigned to us. If we can finish our course triumphantly, like Paul, we shall find blessing all the way, with rich reward at the end.

The time to begin is right now. "Forgetting those things which are behind, and reaching forth unto those things which are before," let us "press toward the mark for the prize of the high calling of God in Christ Jesus" (Phil. 3:13, 14). If the past has been a failure, the future need not be.

Let us heed the exhortation of the apostle Peter, who reminds us that since Christ suffered for us, love and loyalty to Him should lead us to devote our lives to Him. "Forasmuch then as Christ hath suffered for us in the flesh, arm yourselves likewise with the same mind: for he that hath suffered in the flesh hath ceased from sin; that he no longer should live the rest of his time in the flesh to the lusts of men, but to the will of God" (I Pet. 4:1, 2).

3

SOME PERSONAL TESTS

BEFORE WE JUMP TO THE CONCLUSION that we will be ready and willing to do God's will as soon as we find out what it is, it may be profitable for us to search our hearts and see whether this is really true. Probably most of us suppose we would be quick to obey the Lord, if only He would give to us the kind of personal revelation He gave to Elijah or Ezekiel in Old Testament days. Let us not be too hasty in saying this, for it may be possible that a spiritual inventory will reveal a degree of unsuspected unwillingness to serve our Lord. If so, we shall then be in a position to remedy whatever is wrong. The discovery of failure on our part may be the beginning of a life of blessing and success beyond anything we thought could be ours to enjoy.

We are living in an age when everyone may have his own copy of the Word of God, which reveals His will. If we had to depend on a message of fire written across the sky, or the voice of an angel in a dream, we might easily be deceived. Our memories would not perfectly recall the details, nor the first impression of such an event. Instead of communicating His program to us by any such method, God has given us His written Word, wonderfully preserved through the ages since it was inscribed by holy men inspired of God.

Let's Use the "Touchstone"

The Bible contains many plain statements about what the Lord would have us do. It also challenges us to test ourselves by what it teaches. "Examine yourselves, whether ye be in the faith; prove your own selves" (II Cor. 13:5). The original meaning of the language here recalls the method used by ancient assayers to test the purity of gold. They applied a touchstone to it, of jasper or Lydian flint, which revealed whether or not the metal was genuine. Our touchstone is the Word of God. When we apply the Word to ourselves, comparing what it asks of us with what we find in our own hearts, we learn to what degree we are actually honoring the message of God to us.

There are many places in the Scriptures where explicit statements about God's will for His people are to be found. Let us apply some of these as personal tests, for it is evident that if we are not willing to follow the plain instructions the Lord has already given, we have no right to expect further directions for the conduct of our lives. We must be ready to show respect for His words. "The secret of the Lord is with them that fear him; and he will show them his covenant" (Ps. 25:14). Those who really mean business with God are favored with personal guidance from day to day.

1. Separation from Known Sin Is God's Will for Us

"This is the will of God, even your sanctification" (I Thess. 4:3). No one could ask for a plainer statement. Although it is a part of what we have called the general will of God for all His people, it is put in such a way as to supply us with a test case for self-examination.

God is holy. He cannot look on sin with the least degree of allowance. "If I regard iniquity in my heart, the Lord will not hear me" (Ps. 66:18). To cherish some loved sin, and refuse to give it up for Christ's sake, is to erect a barrier between us and the blessings of communion with God. If we are serious about learning His plan for our lives, we must consider this verse as one of His first messages to us. He wills that we shall be sanctified.

It is not necessary for us to stop and examine the details of the great doctrine of sanctification at this point. To be sanctified is to be set apart; this is the literal meaning of the word. We are set apart unto God, in one sense of the term, the moment we receive Christ, for we are bought with the price of His blood. Some day we shall be set apart from sin forever, by being taken to glory with Christ. But I Thessalonians 4:3 speaks of our present responsibility. God wants us to take our stand against every form of known sin, and to maintain that stand consistently. The context of the verse indicates what kinds of sin are immediately in view: sins of impurity (v. 3); greedy desire for something we do not have (v. 5); and fraud of all kinds, which of course includes cheating in school examinations just as much as it does the defrauding of others in business (v. 6).

To enable us to become free from such sins, we have been given the Bible, which sanctifies and cleanses us (Eph. 5:26). Like a mirror, it shows us our shortcomings, and then provides the remedy, so that we may be transformed more and more into the likeness of Christ (II Cor. 3:18). In addition, the Holy Spirit dwells within us to keep us from giving in to the lusts of the flesh (Gal. 5:16). Also, the Lord Jesus "ever liveth to make intercession" for all who have come unto God by Him (Heb. 7:25). Everything has been done to make a clean, godly life possible for the Christian.

2. Prayer and Thanksgiving Are God's Will for Us

"Pray without ceasing. In everything give thanks: for this is the will of God in Christ Jesus concerning you" (I Thess. 5:17, 18). Here is another clear statement, like a voice from heaven answering our question, "Lord, what wilt thou have me to do?"

It is a strange thing, that with more books available on the subject than ever before, prayer is almost a lost art to the present generation. With the riches of the devotional literature of the ages to draw on, people face the most serious kind of trouble without apparently thinking it necessary to spend an hour or two, much less a night, in prayer. It seems almost incredible that we should regard the Word of God so lightly, but it is true.

Pastors frequently find that families have been facing calamities of all kinds, without thinking it necessary to meet with other Christians at the prayer meeting. Missionaries are obliged to face the terrible power of the enemies of the cross without the prayer support that could bring down power from on high, because so many in the homeland forget that one of the main channels God uses for the blessing of His people is their intercession for each other.

To "pray without ceasing" and "in everything give thanks" mean more than offering an occasional prayer at bedtime, or bowing for a moment at lunch. It is to lift our hearts to the Lord constantly throughout every day, in thanksgiving for the abundant evidences of His love, and in earnest petition concerning everything we do, that we may please Him and have His blessing. We do not have to retire to a monastery to be in communion with the Lord during every waking hour.

"In nothing be anxious; but in everything by prayer and supplication with thanksgiving let your requests be made known unto God. And the peace of God, which

passeth all understanding, shall guard your hearts and
your thoughts in Christ Jesus" (Phil. 4:6, 7, R.V.). Perfect
peace about the future, as well as about everything else,
is dependent on our meeting this threefold requirement
calling for *prayer,* which is the ordinary word for continuous communion with God; *supplication,* or the fervent intercession demanded by some situations; and
thanksgiving. When we remember to do this, we have little difficulty deciding whether we are where the Lord
wants us to be.

3. Good Deeds Are God's Will for Us

"For so is the will of God, that with well doing ye may put
to silence the ignorance of foolish men" (I Pet. 2:15). The
world is full of ignorant and foolish people who are quick
to make the most of the failings of Christians. We are
being watched constantly, and so we must be on our
guard, quieting the tongues of the enemies of
Christianity by deeds of kindness and love. We have no
right to give them any ammunition to use against the
cause of Christ with which we are associated.

What forms of well doing are in view? The preceding
verses afford several suggestions. We are to abstain from
fleshly lusts. We are to be transparently honest in
everything. We are to respect the laws of the land, and
the rules of the office or shop where we work. This means
we must be careful not to neglect the work for which an
employer is paying us, even to engage in Christian service
or religious argument. Doubtless, we fulfill the spirit of
I Peter 2:15 when we give to the Red Cross, or engage in
other benevolent enterprises not under the direct control
of the Church. "As we have therefore opportunity, let us
do good unto all men" (Gal. 6:10).

The subject of our good deeds is so important that it is
set forth in the Bible as one reason why God has saved us.

"We are his workmanship, created in Christ Jesus unto good works" (Eph. 2:10). Christ "gave himself for us, that he might redeem us from all iniquity, and purify unto himself a peculiar people, zealous of good works" (Titus 2:14).

If we have been neglecting to put good works in their proper place as part of the divine plan for us, we can easily begin at once to bring our lives into conformity with the Word. There is an extra incentive in the warning of James 4:17: "Therefore to him that knoweth to do good, and doeth it not, to him it is sin." It is not the things we fail to do through ignorance which are here in view, but the things we know we ought to do, and yet neglect. Inactivity then becomes sin.

4. Suffering Is Sometimes God's Will for Us

"Let them that suffer according to the will of God commit the keeping of their souls to him in well doing, as unto a faithful creator" (I Pet. 4:19). Many examples are found in the Scriptures showing why godly people often suffer.

The three Hebrew young men who were cast into the fiery furnace entered into a new experience of the love of God as the result of their trial. They had a personal revelation of His power to deliver them; they walked with Him in the midst of the fire; a divinely given capacity to endure the flame was theirs; the enemies of God were confounded; they became a blessing to multitudes who have since read their story (Dan. 3).

It was because the disciples had followed the Lord Jesus into the ship that they found themselves threatened by a terrific storm on the sea of Galilee (Matt. 8:23-27). He led them into trouble so that they might behold something never before seen by human eyes, the power of His word over the forces of nature.

The blind man in John 9:3 was suffering "that the works of God should be made manifest in him." Because he was born blind, the power of Christ was manifested; both physical and spiritual sight came to him, and the Bible record of his experience has since brought many to the Lord.

When Paul was lashed and then thrown into a dungeon in Philippi, somebody might have said that he must be out of the will of God, or such a thing could not have happened. Yet he had gone to that city because he obeyed a heavenly vision, given while he was risking his life each day as a foreign missionary. Believers still thank God for the stream of blessing which has flowed from that time of suffering (Acts 16:23-31).

God has a purpose in whatever He permits us to know of affliction. "If we suffer, we shall also reign with him" (II Tim. 2:12). If we desire above all else to do God's will, and it is His purpose that we suffer for a time, let us not complain nor rebel, but commit ourselves to Him as unto a faithful Creator who has a reason for everything He does. He has a perfect plan. "Whom the Lord loveth he chasteneth" (Heb. 12:6), but it is for our profit, and it yields "the peaceable fruit of righteousness" afterward (vv. 10, 11).

As we pursue the path He sets before us, we are warned in advance about trouble, and comforted as well. "Beloved, think it not strange concerning the fiery trial which is to try you, as though some strange thing happened unto you: but rejoice, inasmuch as ye are partakers of Christ's sufferings; that, when his glory shall be revealed, ye may be glad also with exceeding joy" (I Pet. 4:12, 13).

Reproach and persecution may come. Does this mean we have missed His plan? Not at all. Rather, if we are reproached for the name of Christ, it means the spirit of glory and of God rests upon us (v. 14). This is enough to turn our sorrow into joy. It is a revelation which should make the thorniest part of our pathway a delight.

4

THE STEPS OF A GOOD MAN

No STATEMENT OF SCRIPTURE about the way God leads His people is more arresting than Psalm 37:23: "The steps of a good man are ordered by the Lord: and he delighteth in his way." Here is a revelation so exceedingly important that it deserves our careful study in the light of its context.

The wonder of this teaching increases when we notice what is really involved. The steps of a good man are *ordered* by the Lord. In the Revised Version this is *established*. The same Hebrew word is translated *ordained* in Psalm 8:3, "the moon and the stars, which thou hast ordained."

The science of astronomy has recorded something of the amazing precision of the movements of the heavenly bodies. Eclipses of the sun and moon, conjunctions of the planets, and other phenomena can be accurately predicted hundreds of years before they occur. A planetarium projects pictures of the sky upon a domed screen which are so perfect that the audience is able to see the stars and planets just as Abraham saw them over the mountains of ancient Palestine, or as they will appear in the distant future. This is possible because God has established a fixed orbit for each one, which can be calculated with the utmost exactitude.

An Ordained Pathway

The same divine wisdom and care that has ordained the movements of the stars of the sky has ordained our steps as children of God! The same power by which the stars are kept in their courses is at the disposal of believers, to keep them in the way of obedience to the plan of God. This is an astonishing revelation, but it is one which reappears in the New Testament. "We are his workmanship, created in Christ Jesus unto good works, which God hath before ordained that we should walk in them" (Eph. 2:10).

There is a word picture in Jude 13 which presents a striking contrast by describing certain among the ungodly as "wandering stars, to whom is reserved the blackness of darkness forever." The symbolism is that of a comet, or some other body from outer space, entering the solar system and the warm light of our sun; then departing on a wandering course farther and farther into outer darkness. True believers, on the other hand, are subject to the governing control of the Sun of righteousness (Mal. 4:2). Christ is the center of the divinely chosen orbit in which they move.

Such a disclosure of the interest God shows in His children is far removed from any philosophy of fatalism. It is not as though each believer were a robot, an automaton acting without any choice of its own. We have been given freedom to accept or to reject the blueprint God offers for the conduct of our lives. A further consideration of Psalm 37 emphasizes this, for not all believers have the right to think of verse 23 as applicable to them. A clear description is given of those concerning whom the statement is made.

The translation of Psalm 37:23 found in the familiar King James Version of the Scriptures is likely to be misunderstood. We read, "The steps of a *good* man are ordered by the Lord." It will be noticed that the word "good" is printed in italics. This means that it does not appear in the original Hebrew text as written by the psalmist. The great scholars who gave us our common version in 1611 were faced with many difficult questions of how best to represent the exact meaning of the Hebrew in our tongue. Where it seemed necessary to add an English word in the interest of clarity or beauty, italics were used to indicate that the word was not found in the original text.

When the translators came to Psalm 37:23, they found an unusual word for man. It has no exact English equivalent. It is used in comparatively few places; in fact, it appears only once previously in the entire Book of Psalms: "O taste and see that the Lord is good: blessed is the man that trusteth in him" (Ps. 34:8). Its true meaning is established by this first use.

"As Many as Received Him . . ."

To say that every good man is under the personal direction of the Lord is obviously wrong. There are good men among unbelievers, but only those who have received Christ are sons of God (John 1:12). The human estimate of goodness is quite different from God's estimate. We are not to suppose that our text speaks merely of any good man, as we might count goodness. It speaks rather of an individual who trusts in the Lord and is surrendered to Him.

One of the very first rules for Bible study is, "Observe the context." That is, we must take into consideration the setting in which we find a verse. A portion of Scripture removed from its place often conveys a meaning quite different from that which was intended. For example, someone might quote Job 2:4 as a text from the Bible and therefore true: "All that a man hath will he give for his life." However, this is an utterance of Satan, the father of lies, and it is not set forth in the Bible as a true statement at all. Many martyrs have proved that they counted their faith dearer than life itself; many parents have died for the sake of their children.

Psalm 37:23, alone, can be misunderstood, since it is only part of an extended description of the faithful people of God. Two men are set over against each other in the context. One is righteous, the other is wicked. One is saved, the other is lost. Even a superficial reading of the entire psalm makes this plain. Out of all the truths there contained, four short exhortations in the opening verses may be selected as a description of the individual whose steps are directed by the Lord. These four portions supply us with an easy test for our own self-examination:

1. "Trust in the Lord, and Do Good" (v. 3)

This is where everyone must begin who seeks divine guidance. The Hebrew word for trusting meant to flee for refuge, and therefore to have confidence in something. We trust in the Lord when we go to Him for refuge from the penalty and power of our sins, to lay hold upon the hope He sets before us (Heb. 6:18).

Anyone who has confidence in his own goodness, so that he thinks he has earned a certain standing before God, has nothing awaiting him in any such passage as this psalm. Its first requirement is trust in the Lord, which means renouncing all trust in self, or personal righteousness, to cast oneself upon the mercy and grace of God.

There are many self-righteous persons in the world. When asked about the basis of their hope for heaven,

they speak of their success in keeping the Ten Commandments, or the Golden Rule. They are doing the best
they can; they love their fellow men; they say they are
better than some church members they know. Instead of
the Bible principle that blood-cleansed sinners go to
heaven, they prefer to believe the world's notion that the
good go to heaven. Not what Christ has done for them,
but what they are doing for themselves and others is the
important thing in their judgment. The words of
Ephesians 2:8, 9 are overlooked: "By grace are ye saved
through faith; and that not of yourselves: it is the gift of
God: not of works, lest any man should boast."

"Trust in the Lord, and do good." This is the right
kind of goodness, since it springs from sincere trust in
Christ. Probably this was what the translators had in
mind when they inserted the word "good" in verse 23.
Native goodness, sometimes called the milk of human
kindness, proves nothing as to a man's salvation. But
when someone tries to do good for the sake of Christ, it
becomes an evidence that his faith is genuine. "Faith
without works is dead" (James 2:20).

Like other eternal truths revealed in the Old
Testament, this is also found in the New Testament. Paul
was commissioned to preach that men "should repent
and turn to God, and do works meet for repentance"
(Acts 26:20). He wrote, "I will that thou affirm constantly, that they which have believed in God might be
careful to maintain good works" (Titus 3:8). Salvation is
a unit. We cannot separate faith from good works, as
though one could be exhibited without the other.

2. "Delight Thyself Also in the Lord; and He
Shall Give Thee the Desires of Thine Heart" (v. 4)

Here is something which follows salvation by faith in
Christ. It is a second step not yet taken by every believer.

All Christians **have** trusted in the Lord, but not all have **delighted** themselves in the One whom they have trusted, **and** the fact that they do not have the desires of their hearts is proof.

What a promise this is! Every desire will be granted to us by the Lord, if we fulfill the single condition mentioned. The fault lies with us alone if this is not our own daily experience. He has never failed to keep His word. He will honor it when we grant to Him our implicit obedience.

Some delight themselves in pleasure. Others find their chief delight in business, or a career, or music, or fishing, or any one of a thousand other things. Obviously, many of these are good and profitable in their proper place. God has given us all the world, brimful of wholesome pleasures, richly for us to enjoy (I Tim. 6:17). It is only when something usurps the place rightfully belonging to the Lord that it becomes sin.

It is not a difficult matter to learn what it means to delight ourselves in the Lord. It is to live so as to please Him, to honor everything we find in His Word, to do everything the way He would like to have it done, and for Him.

The same expression is found in another passage, where its meaning is made clear. "If thou turn away thy foot from the sabbath, from doing thy pleasure on my holy day; and call the sabbath a delight, the holy of the Lord, honorable; and shalt honor him, not doing thine own ways, nor finding thine own pleasure, nor speaking thine own words: then shalt thou delight thyself in the Lord; and I will cause thee to ride upon the high places of the earth, and feed thee with the heritage of Jacob thy father: for the mouth of the Lord hath spoken it" (Isa. 58:13, 14).

Delighting to obey the Lord is thus the same thing as delighting in the Lord Himself. The principle found in this passage may be applied to any other command of the Bible. If we delight in having no other gods before Him, delight in honoring our father and mother, delight in keeping all the teachings of Scripture, we shall be delighting ourselves in Him. "Them that honor me, I will honor" (I Sam. 2:30). This is a law of the spiritual world. If we want to ride upon the high places of the earth, knowing heaven's highest blessings in the fulfillment of every desire of our hearts, here is the secret. We must respect the Scriptures enough to make them our rule of life.

3. "Commit Thy Way unto the Lord; Trust Also in Him; and He Shall Bring It to Pass" (v. 5)

It is fitting that this should be the third admonition of the psalm, because it belongs after the others. Not until we have trusted in Christ as Saviour, then delighted ourselves in Him as Lord, does He speak about taking charge of us and leading us into the fullness of His blessing.

If we have not trusted in Him, we are not yet children of God at all. If we have not delighted ourselves in Him, we have not taken our salvation very seriously, and it is doubtful that we would respond to the guidance He yearns to provide. As long as our own way is so pleasant that we delight in it rather than in Him, we shall not be ready to take the third logical step toward walking in His path.

There is a word picture here. To "commit" is to act like a man who, carrying a burden he is unable to bear, rolls it on the shoulders of someone stronger than himself who is willing to carry his load for him. When we commit our way unto the Lord, we acknowledge that this is our situation. We tell Him we cannot guide our own lives aright, and we entrust them to Him as the One who is able and willing to take complete charge of them.

The remainder of the verse is not to be overlooked. Having completed the act of committing our way unto the Lord, we are to begin a process of continuous trust. Our part in the transaction is not finished when we have decided we want the Lord to direct our steps, and have told Him so at some dedication service.

Necessary as is the act of commitment, it must be followed by obedience to the further words, "trust also in Him." We are to keep on trusting, even though the promised response may seem long in coming from the Lord. It may take considerable time for Him to bring us to the place where we shall be aware of His still, small voice of love. By trusting in Him throughout such a period of necessary heart preparation, we give evidence of the sincerity of our declaration.

The reward of faith is sure: "He shall bring it to pass." God will do what He has promised. He will vindicate His people who have dared to trust Him. Their righteousness and their judgment will some day be recognized by all.

4. "Rest in the Lord and Wait Patiently for Him" (v. 7)

Resting in the Lord means refraining from anxious thought about the future (Matt. 6:34). "The wicked are like the troubled sea, when it cannot rest" (Isa. 57:20). On the contrary, "Thou wilt keep him in perfect peace, whose mind is stayed on thee: because he trusteth in thee" (Isa. 26:3).

It is not always easy, in some circumstances, to decide what is God's plan. Having told Him by acts and words that we mean business with Him, we are to rest quietly in full confidence that He will make the way plain. It is not necessary to jump hastily into the first door which seems to be open.

Verse 34 continues the thought: "Wait on the Lord, and keep his way, and he shall exalt thee." Our true exaltation will take place at His coming, of course, but He will exalt us in this present life. "Humble yourselves therefore under the mighty hand of God, that he may exalt you in due time: casting all your care upon him; for he careth for you" (I Pet. 5:6, 7). Open reward is given for secret prayer (Matt. 6:6).

Let us suppose we have been obeying the four admonitions found at the beginning of Psalm 37, after carefully considering what they mean. But we are conscious of our own weakness, and we hesitate to believe such a wonderful revelation can be true of us, that our steps are established by the Lord in an ordained path. We know we have been guilty of unworthy thoughts, words and acts. Does not our failure to be all the Lord would have us be exclude us from the promise? The wonderful answer is that the following verse recognizes human frailty and infirmity as an element in our walk, and makes provision for it.

His Constant Love

It is written about the trusting, obedient individual described in this psalm that the Lord "delighteth in his way. Though he fall, he shall not be utterly cast down: for the Lord upholdeth him with his hand" (vv. 23, 24). This is language we all can understand. God rejoices in the way we take. When we stumble, like children learning their first steps, He puts us on our feet again. We have seen earthly parents delighting in the efforts being made by their children to walk after their example. The father holds the hand of his small son to guide him. The child is weak. When he stumbles and loses his balance for a moment, he does not come to any serious harm because a stronger hand than his is holding him.

God is our heavenly Father. He watches our steps with great interest and tender compassion. When we fall, in our weakness, He gently restores us to our place, so that we are not utterly cast down. Stern measures may sometimes be required, if we repeatedly demand our own way; but if our delight is in Him (v. 4), then His delight is in us (v. 23).

Thus, our weakness and God's strength are found linked together in what the Bible teaches about His program for our lives. Our tendency to fall is met with His desire to lead us by the hand. "If I take the wings of the morning, and dwell in the uttermost parts of the sea; even there shall thy hand lead me, and thy right hand shall hold me" (Ps. 139:9, 10). The Lord Jesus said of His own, "My Father, which gave them me, is greater than all; and no man is able to pluck them out of my Father's hand" (John 10:29).

David wrote Psalm 37 after a long life, during which he had ample opportunity to observe God's people. He said, "I have been young, and now am old; yet have I not seen the righteous forsaken, nor his seed begging bread" (v. 25). Trials will surely come to us, but our trust is in the Lord. He is our strength in time of trouble (v. 39). He will guide us through every circumstance until we have finished our earthly course.

5

THE THREEFOLD RULE OF EARTH'S WISEST MAN

THE WISDOM OF SOLOMON has always been famous. He wrote the Book of Proverbs, the most remarkable collection of wise sayings in all literature. When his fame began to spread over the whole earth, the Queen of Sheba came to prove him with hard questions. Her judgment was, "The half was not told me: thy wisdom and prosperity exceedeth the fame which I heard" (I Kings 10:7).

The older we get, the more we realize the truth of this position. The Proverbs exceed anything we have ever heard about them, because they are the crystallized wisdom of the wisest man who ever lived. When King Solomon was offered his heart's desire by the Lord, he set riches and honor aside to ask in all humility for "an understanding heart to judge thy people, that I may discern between good and bad" (I Kings 3:9). The gracious response came, "Behold, I have done according to thy words: lo, I have given thee a wise and an understanding heart; so that there was none like thee before thee, neither after thee shall any arise like unto thee" (v. 12).

The Book of Proverbs is God's wisdom communicated to His people to govern their lives on the earth. Great men of God in every generation have borne witness that when they conducted their affairs on the principles set forth in this book, they prospered beyond their expectations. Notable examples of this are known in our day, and this will continue to be the case until the Lord comes.

It is to be expected that such a book contains explicit directions by which young people can determine God's will for them, so that they may follow it from their youth. The very language of Proverbs seems to have been chosen with them in mind. The first seven chapters are plentifully sprinkled with verses which begin with the words, "My son . . ." Most of these chapters open with this form of address, making us feel that God the Father is speaking directly to us as His children. No better advice could be given to young Christians, faced with the wonderful possibilities which life presents, than to make the reading of Proverbs a daily habit.

First Things First

On the threshold of the book is one of the key phrases to understanding the plan of God: "The fear of the Lord is the beginning of knowledge" (Prov. 1:7). Of those who refuse this revelation, it is written, "They hated knowledge, and did not choose the fear of the Lord: they would none of my counsel: they despised all my reproof. Therefore shall they eat of the fruit of their own way, and be filled with their own devices" (1:29-31). It was because people wanted their own way that Christ had to die on the cross (Isa. 53:6). It is because people want their own way that they live unhappy, defeated lives.

Solomon had a great deal to say about right and wrong paths, and the blessings God sends to those who follow where He leads. One statement stands out from all others as a marvel of simplicity and comprehensiveness. It is given the central position among five very practical rules of life found in Proverbs 3:1-10. Each of these is worthy of careful attention.

Long life and peace are promised to those who forget not the law of God, but keep His commandments from the heart (vv. 1, 2). Favor and good understanding in the sight of God and man is the sure portion of those who are characterized by mercy and truth (vv. 3, 4). Health and strength accompany a humble fear of God (vv. 7, 8). Temporal prosperity is offered to all who will honor the Lord with their substance (vv. 9, 10).

Lest someone should be inclined to ask, after years of sincere effort to respect these precepts, Why then do I suffer affliction? they are followed by the revelation that when God the Father chastens His children, it is done in tender love. "My son, despise not the chastening of the Lord; neither be weary of his correction: for whom the Lord loveth he correcteth; even as a father the son in whom he delighteth" (vv. 11, 12). It is *because* we are seeking to honor the preceding verses that our Father takes charge of us, and His care includes such discipline as we may need to prepare us for future service on earth, and for the high place He wants us to occupy in eternity.

The matchless words of Solomon about divine guidance are found enshrined in the heart of this section of the Proverbs: "Trust in the Lord with all thine heart; and lean not unto thine own understanding. In all thy ways acknowledge him, and he shall direct thy paths" (vv. 5, 6). Three conditions are here set forth for us to meet: the first and last are positive, and have to do with the Lord; the central one is negative, and it has to do with ourselves.

1. "Trust in the Lord with All Thine Heart"

This is the same precept we found at the beginning of

Psalm 37:3, but an important phrase is added, "with all thine heart." We know what it is to trust in the Lord, if we are Christians at all. Every believer has already fulfilled the first four words of the verse. But it cannot be said that every believer has obeyed the entire first phrase, by trusting with all his heart.

This becomes apparent when we observe that this whole section is addressed to those who are already children of God by faith. We cannot otherwise understand it. Unbelievers are never told to honor the Lord with their substance (v. 9). Instead, "the sacrifice of the wicked is an abomination to the Lord" (15:8). Nor does the Bible ever speak of the unsaved as sons of the Father whom He chastens because He loves them (v. 12). Rather, some are called "the children of the wicked one" (Matt. 13:38), whose father is the devil (John 8:44).

We are required by these considerations to look upon Proverbs 3:5 as a message to believers, calling on them to carry their trust to the point where it takes possession of their hearts. The first and great commandment of the law was, "Thou shalt love the Lord thy God with all thy heart" (Matt. 22:37). The first rule for knowing God's plan for our lives is that we trust Him with all our hearts.

Such a command is reasonable enough, for any lack of confidence in Him would keep us from entering wholeheartedly into His program. When a ship enters the difficult waters leading to some great inland port, the captain surrenders all control of his vessel to the pilot who knows the way ahead. There must be perfect trust in the pilot's ability. When we go to a strange city and engage a taxicab to take us through the maze of streets to our destination, we entrust ourselves altogether to the driver's knowledge of the way. It would be folly to do otherwise. Likewise, we must be willing to let God take full charge of us.

It must be realized that we cannot reserve any right of

self-will in any matter whatsoever. God's will is best. He has placed all the riches of His wisdom, power and love at our disposal. Therefore, we have no reason for being concerned about the future.

Sometimes Christians trust the Lord up to a certain point, but they become frightened into a desperate attempt to force an issue when the pathway seems to get dark. There is no necessity for our trying to break open a door somewhere, when God's moment for an open door has not yet come. He will fulfill all His Word. When we cleave to the Lord with purpose of heart, He responds in such a way as to exceed our expectations, after the period of testing has ended.

2. "Lean Not unto Thine Own Understanding"

Trust in the Lord must not only be entire; it must be exclusive as well. As soon as we trust in ourselves, our hearts have departed from the Lord (Jer. 17:5). There is no room for confidence in the flesh in the life of faith. The human understanding has been darkened ever since sin came into the world (Eph. 4:18). It is not a dependable guide apart from God.

This warning does not mean that there is no place for the intelligent exercise of good judgment, of course. There are many precepts regarding the cultivation of the understanding (Prov. 2:3; 4:7). Christ opened the understanding of His disciples on the resurrection day (Luke 24:45). Paul prayed that the eyes of the understanding of the Ephesian Christians might be enlightened (Eph. 1:18). The teaching of Proverbs 3:5 is that we should not depend solely upon this human faculty.

There may be two courses of action open to us. One of them appears to be very desirable. It has advantages which are easy to see. The other one presents difficulties and may even involve hardship; but it is in keeping with the plain teaching of the Bible, while the other is not.

Then we must not, we dare not, do what our unenlightened understanding may dictate. We must do what the Word indicates is best for us spiritually, no matter how attractive something else may be temporally. We cannot see ahead, but the Lord can. We do not know all the factors; He does. He will vindicate our course later if we trust Him and refuse to lean on our own judgment apart from the Word.

A young man with a splendid voice, which he was using for the Lord on the radio, was offered a position in Hollywood, where his talents would have brought him a large income and great popularity. Knowing that to accept would mean using his voice for worldly gain in a questionable enterprise, and at the price of setting a bad example for other young Christians, he refused. There can be no doubt that he did the right thing, as judged by the Word and in view of eternity. The world would count him foolish now, but the day will come when the whole universe will know that he was wise. In the meanwhile, he has a satisfaction which money can never buy.

A difficult problem facing young people in high school is the question of which college to attend. The choice may be between a famous center of learning and culture, where infidel teachers scoff at the Bible, and a small college where the faculty is made up of men of God. The understanding might favor the big university because of the high standing it gives its graduates, but this must not be made the sole consideration. In pagan universities, some young people have been known to lose their faith, while others have emerged the stronger for their contacts with unbelief and new points of view. A decision to attend such an institution should not be made until it is certain that one is sufficiently well grounded in the Word to be beyond the reach of skeptics and the specious claims of false theories.

Intelligent faith has nothing to fear from scientific facts, but there is danger when a young person who has had no real teaching of Bible truth secures his education from men who take every opportunity to attack the Scriptures. It need hardly be said that the presence of scoffers in some colleges should not result in any lowering of the educational standards of evangelical Christians. God places no premium on ignorance. His Word admonishes us to gain knowledge and wisdom with diligence (Prov. 4:5-9; 22:29). Our testimony carries more weight when we have done this by carefully preparing ourselves.

Leaning on an unenlightened understanding is quite a different thing from the prayerful use of the faculties God has given us to determine His will. He never asks us to abandon all sound judgment. When we are subject to His Word, our understanding is illumined so that it recognizes the wisdom of His plan as it unfolds, and we give our intelligent approval. Human vision is shortsighted. Outward appearances are not always encouraging, but the Lord wants us to have quiet assurance and peace, no matter how dark the future may seem (Isa. 32:17).

3. "In All Thy Ways Acknowledge Him"

This is a familiar thought to every Christian. "Whosoever therefore shall confess me before men, him will I confess also before my Father which is in heaven" (Matt. 10:32). "If thou shalt confess with thy mouth the Lord Jesus, and shalt believe in thine heart that God hath raised him from the dead, thou shalt be saved" (Rom. 10:9). These verses speak of the present assurance and future destiny of those who acknowledge Christ as Saviour. Proverbs 3:6, on the other hand, speaks of the continuous guidance provided for those who acknowledge Him in all their ways as they try to serve Him in everyday life.

We are thus confessing Him when we let everyone with whom we come in contact know we have made Him our Saviour and Lord. This does not mean talking about Him in an ostentatious way wherever we happen to be. We do not have to carry a banner on a stick through a crowded city street to be faithful representatives of Christ, nor is it necessary for us to force ourselves on those we meet. He will give us opportunities to speak to hearts He has already prepared, if we make this a matter of definite daily prayer.

To acknowledge Him in all our ways is to show by our actions, as much as our words, what He has come to mean to us. The world is able to see whether we are bearing the fruit of the Spirit, "love, joy, peace, longsuffering, gentleness, goodness, faith, meekness, temperance" (Gal. 5:22). People notice it when we refuse to have any part in things a Christian should not do. The way we live, the places we go, the company we keep, all form a part of our public witness for the Lord. These alone, however, are hardly sufficient if we remain silent when Christ needs a true witness, whether it be in reproach of sin or the positive affirmation of the gospel.

Those who work with aromatic wood carry the perfume with them unconsciously wherever they go. In the days of the early disciples, "they took knowledge of them, that they had been with Jesus" (Acts 4:13). This ought to be true of us, not because of any boasting display of sanctity, but because the fragrance of the Lord Jesus permeates everything we do, since we are so much in His presence.

We are acknowledging the Lord when we go to Him for counsel about all our ways. Every step is to be taken under His direction. His wisdom ought to guide us even in small matters. He loves to be consulted by those who trust Him. We are not to suppose that any circumstance is so clear as to make this unnecessary. Even Joshua made a serious mistake when he "asked not counsel at the mouth of the Lord," in the matter of the Gibeonites (Josh. 9:14). Whether the way be clear or dark, we are to acknowledge our dependence upon Him.

These are the three simple rules given by God through Solomon as the secret of divine guidance. Other Scripture passages elaborate them, but these three things are fundamental. When we observe them in all sincerity, we have the guarantee, "He shall direct thy paths." The Lord will take full charge of us. The promise could not be more specific.

If we are not at the moment in the place He wants us to be, we may rest assured that He will lead us out of our present position into the place of His choosing. In the meanwhile, "Let every man abide in the same calling wherein he was called" (I Cor. 7:20). In God's own time, when He sees that we are ready, we shall be led into the work He has intended us to do for Him.

6

CHRIST AND THE
WILL OF GOD

THE LIFE OF THE LORD JESUS CHRIST presents us with a perfect illustration of absolute conformity to the will of God. We are not likely to realize how important a place this is given in the record of His ministry, until we bring together a number of scriptures devoted to it. No study of the God-planned life would be complete which omitted some reference to the way it was exemplified in Christ.

When Peter wrote of the Lord as our Example, he used a remarkable word found nowhere else in the Bible. "Christ also suffered for us, leaving us an *example,* that ye should follow his steps" (I Pet. 2:21). In the Greek language this was *hypogrammos,* an expression familiar enough to the schoolrooms of ancient Greece. It was what they called the line of script placed at the top of a page for the children to copy in their writing exercises. It contained all the letters of the alphabet, providing a perfect standard by which the work of each child could be guided and judged.

Similar copybooks, with samples of beautiful English script, are used in our own country today, so that this word is full of meaning. It teaches us that we are to be like school children in our relationship to Christ. He is our Example; we are to reproduce His character before the world. When we receive Him as Saviour, the fresh open page of the future lies before us. It is our happy task to show forth His grace, and sweetness, and love to those about us.

At first, our attempts may be comparable with the crude scrawls of all beginners, for we are "babes in Christ" (I Cor. 3:1). But soon we begin to grow in knowledge (II Pet. 3:18), in obedience to the command, "As newborn babes, desire the sincere milk of the word, that ye may grow thereby" (I Pet. 2:2). We become "wise unto salvation" (II Tim. 3:15), and normally, we become more Christlike. When we have finally reached the bottom of the page of our earthly lives, we should be giving evidence that we have kept our Example before us always, "for even hereunto were ye called."

Every Bible teaching about the Christian life finds in Christ its perfect embodiment. We see exemplified in Him all we can find written about prayer, and love, and holiness, for example. It is our present purpose to notice how He illustrates the subject of undeviating conformity to the will of the Father. No matter where we look, we find Him entirely subject to the divine program.

1. In His Life Purpose

One of the plainest revelations about the object for which the Lord left glory and came to earth is found in the discourse on the bread of life: "I came down from heaven, not to do mine own will, but the will of him that sent me" (John 6:38).

A much earlier statement appears in Hebrews 10:5-10, which begins with the astonishing words, "When he cometh into the world, he saith, Sacrifice and offering thou wouldest not, but a body hast thou prepared me." Every effort to get rid of the plain meaning of this verse by those who deny the pre-existence and the deity of our Lord, has failed. He came into the world at His incarnation when He was born in Bethlehem of Judea. As a baby in the manger, He was no less conscious of the purpose of His coming than when He was teaching His disciples about the necessity for the cross.

The subject of this conversation between God the Father and God the Son when He came into the world was the purpose He was to accomplish with the body prepared for Him. Throughout the history of the human race, burnt offerings and sacrifices for sin were offered, but they could not cancel sin (Heb. 10:6). Then came the night on which Christ was born, and He said, "Lo, I come (in the volume of the book it is written of me,) to do thy will, O God" (v. 7).

What was the nature of God's will for His Son? The answer is found in verse 10, "By the which will we are sanctified through the offering of the body of Jesus Christ once for all." He was born to die. This is why He came, so that we might be set apart unto God through His death on Calvary.

There is a definite parallel between Christ and those who follow Him. We, too, have the privilege of knowing that we are to fulfill an eternal destiny, being "predestinated according to the purpose of him who worketh all things after the counsel of his own will" (Eph. 1:11). The word "predestinated" simply means our destiny has been determined beforehand by the God who has called us according to His purpose, and who foreknew everything about us, including the fact that we would receive His Son as Saviour (Rom. 8:28, 29).

We open the Bible and read, "He hath chosen us in him before the foundation of the world" (Eph. 1:4), or, "God hath from the beginning chosen you" (II Thess. 2:13). It is a source of wonder and inspiration to learn these things. The only fitting response is for us to echo the words of Christ our Example, "I delight to do thy will, O my God" (Ps. 40:8).

2. In the Days of His Youth

The Scriptures reveal but one incident in the life of the Lord Jesus during the thirty years intervening between His early childhood and the opening of His public ministry. Yet that single reference contains evidence that Jesus was doing His Father's will even as a boy.

When He was twelve years old, His parents found Him in the Temple at Jerusalem among the doctors of the law. Questioned about what He had been doing, He replied, "Wist ye not that I must be about my Father's business?" (Luke 2:49).

One of the reasons why this story has been included in the brief New Testament record of the life of Christ is its value as a testimony to young believers. It sets before us, in the person of our Example, the possibility of young people living as the Father would have them live, even during school days. "Remember now thy Creator in the days of thy youth" (Eccles. 12:1).

3. In Every Relationship

In relation to the Scriptures, the Lord Jesus esteemed the words of the Father more than His necessary food. When His disciples wondered how He could be more interested in winning a lost soul than in refreshing His body when hungry, He said, "My meat is to do the will of him that sent me, and to finish his work" (John 4:34).

In relation to others, Christ placed those who do God's will on a higher plane than His earthly brothers, sisters and mother. The new relationship existing between Him and all who respect the Word of God as He did, is so real, so important, that it goes far beyond anything known by those who had been brought up under the same roof with Him in Nazareth. "For whosoever shall do the will of my

Father which is in heaven, the same is my brother, and sister, and mother" (Matt. 12:50; cf. Mark 6:3). This brings Him very close to all of us; it promises a communion with Him of surpassing sweetness.

In relation to prayer, the Lord sought nothing outside the purpose for which God had sent Him. We are taught by Him to pray in like manner as He did, "Thy will be done in earth, as it is in heaven" (Matt. 6:10). Such a petition implies willingness to do our part in bringing about that for which we pray. It includes the thought, "Thy will be done in me." Active obedience is something quite different from the mere repetition of a prayer which is not really understood. "Not every one that saith unto me, Lord, Lord, shall enter into the kingdom of heaven; but he that doeth the will of my Father which is in heaven" (Matt. 7:21).

In relation to the kingdom of God, Christ taught that it is made up of those who are willingly subject to God's will. He used the parable of the two sons, one of whom actually obeyed his father, and one who did not, despite the best of intentions (Matt. 21:28-32). When people with a background of sin and rebellion against God repent and do His will, like the first son and like "the publicans and harlots" of verse 31, they go into the kingdom of God, while the willful self-righteous remain outside. The Father's will is that all who honor the word of His Son shall have everlasting life in the kingdom, and be raised at the last day (Matt. 13:43; John 6:39, 40).

4. In Words and Deeds

The Lord Jesus never said one word which came from His own will as separate from the Father's. "My doctrine is not mine, but his that sent me" (John 7:16). "The word which ye hear is not mine, but the Father's" (14:24). We must learn that our tongues need to be controlled by the Holy Spirit (James 3:6). If we follow Christ's example in this, we shall be guilty of "neither filthiness, nor foolish talking, nor jesting" (Eph. 5:4), which are three expressions denoting any form of speech which tends toward sin. God is able to set a watch before our mouths, and to keep the door of our lips (Ps. 141:3).

Christ never did anything apart from the Father. His deeds were "the works which the Father hath given me to finish" (John 5:36). In fact, He said, "I do nothing of myself; but as my Father hath taught me" (8:28). In like manner, all our actions are governed by the command, "Whatsoever ye do in word or deed, do all in the name of the Lord Jesus, giving thanks to God and the Father by him" (Col. 3:17).

For Christ, this meant the renunciation of all self-will and of all seeking for His own glory. It means no less for us. He has given the example, "I seek not mine own will, but the will of the Father which hath sent me" (John 5:30); "I seek not mine own glory" (8:50).

To follow Him in this means rich gain, rather than loss. It brings to us something of the joy of communion with the Father that Christ knew. "The Father hath not left me alone; for I do always those things that please him" (John 8:29; 16:32). Nor will God leave us alone if we strive to please Him. The planned pathway is never a lonely one, so far as fellowship with the Lord is concerned. "If a man love me, he will keep my words: and my Father will love him, and we will come unto him, and make our abode with him" (John 14:23).

5. In Suffering and Death

Peter's reference to Christ as our Example is placed in a section of his epistle dealing with suffering. It is followed by two references to believers' suffering according to the will of God (I Pet. 3:17; 4:19). We are said to be "partakers of Christ's sufferings" because we are members of His body, and we must live in a world which crucified

Him and is antagonistic to all who belong to Him (John 16:33).

In Christ we find the proper Christian attitude toward affliction. Although He had devoted Himself to becoming sin for us, His holy nature shrank from the dreadful prospect. His prayer in Gethsemane was, "Father, if thou be willing, remove this cup from me: nevertheless not my will, but thine, be done" (Luke 22:42). This must sometimes be our own prayer. If God will, He is able to deliver us from impending trouble; but if not, we know His will is best. That which has been planned and permitted by divine love and wisdom should be acceptable to us. A good example of how we ought to regard trying circumstances is found in Daniel 3:17, 18.

When Christ was born, a definite program lay before Him. Throughout His life, He labored to "finish his work" (John 4:34; 5:36). The moment at last arrived when the end was in sight. He was nailed to the cross. As the whole prophetic outline of His earthly ministry came before Him on Calvary, He knew that one phrase of what had been written still awaited fulfillment.

In Psalm 69:21 it had been prophesied, "In my thirst they gave me vinegar to drink." Vinegar had been offered to Him once, but before the burning thirst of crucifixion was upon Him (Luke 23:36). Parched at last with thirst, "Jesus knowing that all things were now accomplished, that the scripture might be fulfilled, saith, I thirst" (John 19:28). His regard for the Word continued to the end. The agony of Calvary did not cause Him to forget for a moment His purpose to do God's perfect will.

It was when Jesus had received the vinegar that He said, "It is finished: and he bowed his head, and gave up his spirit" (John 19:30, A.S.V.). Much has been written to develop the thought of what was finished at His death. Our salvation was an accomplished fact; its righteous basis was now provided. Satan's defeat was sure; the power of sin was broken. But the thing of importance to our present study is that Christ finished what He had come to do, in fulfilling God's will. An example was now set before the people of God wherein they could see embodied everything written about the God-planned life.

In Christ we see perfectly exemplified the four statements from the Scriptures by which we have tested ourselves as to our willingness to follow where He leads. Christ was separate from sin; He prayed without ceasing; He went along doing good; He suffered according to the will of God. He illustrated the precepts of the Thirty-seventh Psalm by trusting in the Father, delighting Himself in Him, committing His way unto Him, and resting in Him. He personified the wisdom of Solomon by trusting the Father with all His heart, leaning not unto His own understanding, and acknowledging Him in all His ways.

The fact that the Lord Jesus is the only person who has ever perfectly done God's will from birth to death does not in any sense lessen the value of the things we observe in His life. The revelation that He did all these things without sin, having no inborn tendency to self-will, does not make His example any less useful to us. In fact, it is through Him, and through Him only, that we have hope of walking well pleasing to God. He dwells in our hearts by faith. He enables us by His gracious Spirit, by the power He supplies, to face the future, knowing that it is possible for us faithfully to carry out God's program for our own lives.

7

IMPORTANT NEW TESTAMENT TEACHINGS

THERE ARE A GREAT MANY PASSAGES in the New Testament dealing with the will of God. A few of these have already been noticed, since they were anticipated in the Old Testament. It will be profitable to bring together a number of others as illustrating important general principles having to do with the God-planned life, before considering what may be termed definite rules for discovering the divine program for us as individuals.

1. We Do Not Know the Future

When Paul sailed from Ephesus he said to his friends, "I will return again unto you, if God will" (Acts 18:21). It was his desire at another time to go to Corinth and help the church there, but his plans were made subject to his Lord's program, so he wrote, "I will come to you shortly, if the Lord will" (I Cor. 4:19). Again, he said, "I trust to tarry a while with you, if the Lord permit" (I Cor. 16:7). The same restraint is to be seen in his epistle to the church at Rome (Rom. 1:10; 15:32).

We have no more right than Paul to declare in the

presence of others that it is God's will for us to do a certain thing, or to go to a certain place, until it has been made unmistakably clear. There is a modern boldness in this matter which does not give due consideration to repeated statements in the New Testament. In spite of the fact that Paul often used the expression, "if God will," some are heard today declaring that such a phrase indicates lack of faith. There is a place where faith becomes presumption. It is possible to confuse one's own will with that of the Lord. Saying that one is going to be healed of a disease, or that one is called of God to do a certain work, may be nothing more than a pitiful attempt to convince oneself of the presence of a faith which has no real existence.

James warned against any departure from Paul's humility and good sense in this respect when he wrote, "Ye ought to say, If the Lord will, we shall live, and do this, or that" (James 4:15). It is not always God's will for a believer to have abounding physical health, or a large income, or long life. Those who have had some wonderful personal revelation of the power of Christ to heal or to provide or to guide are usually those who have been much in secret prayer rather than much in public protestation about the matter.

Since God leads us step by step, without unveiling large vistas of what lies ahead for us, we must be willing to leave our future entirely in His hands. If we knew too much of His plan, forthcoming joys and privileges might make the present seem drab and unattractive; impending troubles and sorrows would certainly make us unhappy.

Lack of knowledge of the future need not disturb us at any time for "our sufficiency is of God" (II Cor. 3:5). There is a present ministry of the Holy Spirit designed to overcome our inability to select our own path, or to choose what is best. "We know not what we should pray for as we ought: but the Spirit himself maketh intercession for us with groanings which cannot be uttered. And he that searcheth the hearts knoweth what is the mind of the Spirit, because he maketh intercession for the saints according to the will of God" (Rom. 8:26, 27). To this provision may be added the prayers of other believers (Col. 1:9; 4:12), and the privilege of going to the Lord ourselves for guidance (Rom. 1:10).

2. No Man Can Say What God's Will Is for Someone Else

Vocational guidance has its place in discovering natural talents which may be developed, or opportunities which should be seized. But no young people's counselor has either the wisdom or the right to advise a believer in specific terms as to the work God has called him to do. Only the Lord is able perfectly to fit a personality and a life work together.

There is always a place for sound counsel by men of God; "he that hearkeneth unto counsel is wise" (Prov. 12:15). Pastoral advice to young people is doubtless provided for in Hebrews 13:7, 17: "Remember them which have the rule over you, who have spoken unto you the word of God: whose faith follow, considering the end of their conversation [the object of their life] . . . Obey them that have the rule over you, and submit yourselves: for they watch for your souls, as they that must give account." However, since we all have direct access to God, the New Testament is almost silent on this subject. The counsel of godly Christians is of value, but the question of what a young person is to do as a life work must be settled between the individual and God. When Paul's friends in Caesarea endeavored to keep him from going to Jerusalem, where serious trouble awaited him, he was obliged to reject their counsel, and they "ceased, saying, The will of the Lord be done" (Acts 21:13, 14).

A church may discern that the hand of God has been laid upon someone for a particular service, so that one man is granted a place of leadership, and another is sent forth as a missionary; but it is the Holy Spirit who calls people to the work they are to do, and moves in such a way that they are separated unto that work (Acts 13:2, 3).

3. Our Co-operation Is Necessary

God does not force His program on His people beyond the limits suggested in such verses as I Corinthians 11:31, 32, which explain why the chastening of God is sometimes necessary. "For if we would judge ourselves, we should not be judged. But when we are judged, we are chastened of the Lord, that we should not be condemned with the world."

Our co-operation with the divine program is required, "for we are laborers together with God" (I Cor. 3:9). We are admonished, "Work out your own salvation with fear and trembling. For it is God which worketh in you both to will and to do of his good pleasure" (Phil. 2:12, 13). Although some have read only the first part of this portion of Scripture, and have supposed that it calls on Christians to work *for* their salvation, the passage plainly teaches that since God is working within us to bring about His own will through us, we must produce outward evidences of the inward salvation which the Holy Spirit has wrought.

From the moment we receive Christ, God begins to dwell in our hearts (II Cor. 6:16), and to work in such a way as to make us want to do His pleasure rather than our own. We may refuse to co-operate with the indwelling Holy Spirit, but when we submit to His leading we become living examples of the realization of the idea set forth in Hebrews 13:20, 21: "God . . . make you perfect in every good work to do his will, working in you that which is well pleasing in his sight, through Jesus Christ."

The surrender of all self-will is a necessary prelude to our knowing God's program. Those who have the attitude that they will see what God's plan for them is, and then decide whether or not to adopt it, are defeating any prospect of learning the divine program. Willingness to do what God wants us to do is a basic secret of knowing His will and receiving His blessing.

Several Scripture passages illustrate the truth of this. Self-surrender is placed first in Romans 12:1, 2. In Malachi 3:10, God first requires submission to His Word, and then promises, "Prove me now herewith, saith the Lord of hosts, if I will not open you the windows of heaven, and pour you out a blessing, that there shall not be room enough to receive it." Christ said in Matthew 6:33, "Seek ye first the kingdom of God, and his righteousness; and all these things shall be added unto you."

The man who says, "Lord, bless my business and I will give to Thy work out of the proceeds," is putting the cart before the horse. We may not dictate the conditions under which we shall be willing to obey the Lord. In all things He must have the pre-eminence (Col. 1:18).

4. Ample Provision Is Made for Our Own Initiative

It must not be supposed that seeking and following God's plan means the giving up of our own initiative. The person who does his life work as unto Christ will be "not slothful in business; fervent in spirit; serving the Lord" (Rom. 12:11). Laziness is dealt with throughout the Bible in very plain language (Prov. 24:30-34). Every virtue is extolled. Energetic action appears in many phrases: "abounding in the work of the Lord" (I Cor. 15:58); "not

weary in well doing" (Gal. 6:9); "fruitful in every goo
work" (Col. 1:10); "abound more and more" (I Thess
4:1).

The empire builders of the Orient gave way to th
lethargy afterward seen in China and other easter
nations, because they adopted a religion of fatalism
Believing they had no control of their ultimate fate, the
refused to act on their own initiative, but awaited Nir
vana instead. There is a modern doctrine called deter
minism which is producing the same result today amon
those who hold they are not responsible for what they d
because they are creatures of their environment.

How far above such shortsighted, pagan concepts i
the Bible teaching about divine guidance! It requires th
active co-operation of every human faculty, and call
forth the best that is in man by providing the incentive
he needs. We know that God cares for us, plans a won
derful life for us, confirms His plan by providential cir
cumstances, rewards us now and afterward for devotin
our energies to doing the work He has given us to do.

Instead of waiting supinely for what is sometime
called "a leading," the Spirit-filled Christian i
redeeming the time, seizing every opportunity, makin
the most of his gifts, pressing forward, seeking new way
to carry on effectively for his Lord. In the words of Isaia
54:2, 3, he is enlarging the place of his tent, lengthenin
his cords, strengthening his stakes, in preparation fo
breaking forth on the right hand and the left, an
inheriting the Gentiles, whose salvation he seeks. Ever
time a new movement for God has been born, it ha
sprung from one man, or from a few individuals, devote
to the doing of God's perfect will.

5. There Is No Limit to What We Can Accomplish

Probably no one has ever made the most of hi

possibilities. We know this is usually true in school, and in our daily work, and it is also true of our Christian experience. Suppose we have hitherto missed God's plan for us. This does not mean that we are obliged now to take an inferior second or third best plan, for the Lord always has awaiting us His very best. It is never too late to enter into the fullness of His blessing by beginning to do what He wants us to do.

There was a drunkard, not many years ago, who was on his way to drown himself as a hopeless wreck, when he was saved by the power of Christ. It was not long before he was nationally known for the extensiveness and power of his peculiar ministry to outcasts. He founded rescue missions all over America. Nor is his case unique. Every city has its people who achieved success in various occupations because they turned themselves over to Christ. Who shall say there is a limit to what God can do through someone who has missed God's best through many years?

God is able to make a world-wide blessing of anyone who is wholly subject to Him. He is "able to do exceeding abundantly above all that we ask or think, according to the power that worketh in us" (Eph. 3:20). The most remarkable thing about this is not what it says about God's ability, but what it says about the condition by which His exceeding abundant goodness is bestowed upon us. When we allow His power to work in us, there is absolutely no limit to what He may do through us.

Present circumstances must not be permitted to discourage us. Others may have a better education, a more attractive personality, a handsomer face or figure, a stronger voice, a better memory, a keener intellect, a larger amount of time for study, more money, better clothes, influential friends, more good books, or larger opportunities to advance in their chosen vocation. Not one of these things matters very much. We have the en-

couraging words, "I can do all things through Christ
which strengtheneth me" (Phil. 4:13).

America is the place where farm boys may become
President, and where obscure people rise to places of
leadership of all kinds. What is true of our nation is more
wonderfully true of the kingdom of God, wherein even
the giving of a cup of cold water for the sake of Christ
brings a reward (Mark 9:41). "Seest thou a man diligent
in his business? he shall stand before kings; he shall not
stand before mean men" (Prov. 22:29). David among the
sheep and Elisha following the plough were just as much
in God's place for them as when they were later elevated
to positions of honor.

Present outward appearances have nothing to do with
what God may have planned for us. Not often are we
given a great work to do until we have proved ourselves in
a small work. When we take the step just ahead, God will
open the way a bit farther. When we fill the place in
which we find ourselves now, we thereby prove we are fit
to be trusted with greater responsibilities. The faithful
discharge of our present task will often become the
means to an open door leading to a greater work.

6. No Two Believers Have the Same Work to Do

"There are diversities of gifts . . . but all these worketh
that one and the selfsame Spirit, dividing to every man
severally as he will" (I Cor. 12:4, 11). By the sovereign
choice of the Holy Spirit, various gifts are given to us. No
one has every gift, but by the faithful use of what we do
possess, we may expect greater ones. We are to "covet
earnestly the best gifts" (I Cor. 12:31); to "desire
spiritual gifts" (14:1). The most unpromising people have
achieved notable success because they proved themselves
faithful, whether they were teachers or leaders within the
church, or merely "helps" (I Cor. 12:28), that is, men and

women carrying on their business or profession or daily tasks solely as the best way they knew to help the work of the Lord.

Since there are various gifts, some believers achieve more prominence in the world than others. There may be a great musician, a famous statesman, a noted artist, or a successful merchant in the graduating class of some school. The other graduates may face comparative mediocrity in the sight of the world. What then happens to the teaching about the God-planned life? The answer is that there is no mediocrity, no service of little value, in the sight of God. Some who are prominent now will be obscure for eternity; some who are unknown to men now will finally be highly honored (Luke 13:30).

Young people need to be cautioned against imitating others who are in the public eye. Let us have faith in our own significance. It is better to be a voice than an echo. When Peter was too much concerned with what John was to do, the Lord said to him, "What is that to thee? follow thou me" (John 21:22). We all have unrealized potentialities, which may remain unsuspected and untapped if we try to copy someone else.

We must realize that the person who imagines he could be a greater success if he could only step into a larger, established work, or who thinks he could do better if he occupied a position held by someone else, is revealing an unhealthy, morbid attitude. God can be trusted to give our native abilities full play, to make a place for our particular combination of talents. "A man's gift maketh room for him, and bringeth him before great men" (Prov. 18:16).

When we do willingly what God wants us to do, our reward is sure (I Cor. 9:17), although "ye have need of patience, that, after ye have done the will of God, ye might receive the promise" (Heb. 10:36). God is looking for those today about whom He will be able to say, as He said about David, "I have found David the son of Jesse, a man after mine own heart, which shall fulfill all my will" (Acts 13:22). We may not be of kingly stature in this life, but God has chosen us that we should know His will (Acts 22:14), and "faithful is he that calleth you, who also will do it" (I Thess. 5:24).

7. Our Eternal Rewards Depend on Present Faithfulness

In the parable found in Matthew 25:14-30, Christ explained something about this matter of varying gifts, a subject which has troubled many Christians who look upon themselves as "one talent" people. The Lord has given His servants talents, "to every man according to his several ability" (v. 15). But when we stand before Him at His return, He will reward us solely on the basis of the way we have used the gifts we actually possessed. The quality or size of our talents will not be the issue. A five-talent man will receive precisely the same reward as a two-talent man, if both have been equally faithful (vv. 21, 23).

Still, it is evident that some of God's children are truer to their trust than others. How will this be handled in the day of the judgment seat of Christ? The answer is found in the parable of Luke 19:11-27, where each servant is depicted as possessing just one pound. Whereas Matthew 25 views our varying gifts as they appear to men, Luke 19 views them as God sees them, and each man's gift is equally important.

The comparison is therefore based on what the several servants did with the work the Lord gave them to do. Verse 13 is literally, "Carry on business until I come." The one who does his Lord's will most faithfully receives the highest reward. A pound becomes a city. Servants become rulers. Perfect justice is finally done. The principle is, "Thou hast been faithful over a few things, I will make thee ruler over many things." We may count on the Lord's fitting our eternal reward to the degree of faithfulness to Him which we have demonstrated during our life on the earth. "Shall not the Judge of all the earth do right?" Our success in the eyes of men may not have been very great, but when the Lord comes, bringing His reward with Him, it will not be our success, but our faithfulness, which will be the measure of what He bestows on us as our eternal reward.

8

DISCOVERING GOD'S WILL

HAVING CONSIDERED the major passages of Scripture which deal with the subject of God's will, as it applies to the daily life of a believer, it is necessary to gather together the more important truths of the Bible into a simple, comprehensive and practical series of rules by which any sincere Christian can discover for himself God's plan for his life.

The central New Testament teaching about the subject is found in Romans 12:1, 2, which presents a summary of what the Lord expects of us, and an appeal based on His love and mercy. "I beseech you therefore, brethren, by the mercies of God, that ye present your bodies a living sacrifice, holy, acceptable unto God, which is your reasonable service. And be not conformed to this world: but be ye transformed by the renewing of your mind, that ye may prove what is that good, and acceptable, and perfect, will of God."

Notice that this is an earnest entreaty, not a command. We can resist God's pleadings if we choose, but we shall suffer loss now and forever, if we do. He yearns for our glad and willing service. He bases His appeal on what He has already done for us. It is "by the mercies of God," so completely described in the earlier chapters of the Book of Romans. Romans 12:1, 2 is addressed to true believers who appreciate how great is their salvation, and who will therefore respond to the call of God.

Three distinct elements appear. As in Proverbs 3:5, 6, the first and third are positive, while the second is negative. We are to present our bodies to God, to refrain from world conformity, and to be transformed. The thoughtful student will observe a striking similarity between Solomon's threefold rule and this New Testament counterpart. Trust in God is to be entire, exclusive and transfiguring. It yields definite results. God will direct our path, and we shall on our part prove how good, acceptable and perfect is His will for us.

At the threshold of this passage stands an act of dedication by which we turn our bodies over to God, once and for all, to be His for whatever purpose He may have for us. Christ completed His work as a dying sacrifice. He now needs living sacrifices for His present work.

Our act of dedication is to lead to a process of continuous yieldedness to the Lord, described by three terms. As living sacrifices, we must of necessity have renounced self-interest and self-will. As holy, we must be free from known sin. As acceptable to God, we must be of use to Him, submitting to what His Word teaches in our life and work. It is indeed only reasonable that we should comply with His request.

"Be not conformed to this world." We live in a world and in an age that have rejected Christ. There is nothing around us which can give us real peace, joy or satisfaction apart from the Lord. Therefore, we are warned against conforming our lives to the pattern supplied by the world, when we have in Christ the pattern given by God.

"Be ye transformed by the renewing of your mind." The three other places in the New Testament where the word occurs, here rendered "transformed," give us the key to its meaning. Matthew 17:2 and Mark 9:2 use the term of the transfiguration of Christ. Even now, we are to live transfigured lives as citizens of heaven in communion with the Father in glory. II Corinthians 3:18 tells how this may be achieved. We are to keep beholding Christ in the mirror of the Word, and then the Spirit will make us like Him. This is not an external action produced by our keeping a set of rules, but an inward renewing by the Holy Spirit as the mind dwells on spiritual and heavenly things, rather than things of the earth (II Cor. 4:18).

The sure result is that we are able to "prove what is that good, and acceptable, and perfect, will of God." We discover for ourselves God's particular plan for us, and we also demonstrate to the world around, as well as to our own satisfaction, that God's will is everything the Word of God claims for it. Instead of shrinking from His will as something to be feared, we come to recognize joyfully that everything He plans for His children is born of His love, and His desire for our greatest good. We know that all things work together for our blessing, for we love Him and are called according to His purpose (Rom. 8:28).

FIVE PRACTICAL RULES

Most Christians who believe that the plan of their biography is God's have certain favorite portions of Scripture laid away in their hearts for their guidance. We have seen how plentifully such brief summaries of truth are sprinkled throughout the Bible. It is well, however, to provide ourselves also with a few brief rules which bring together the leading principles by which anyone may determine the will of God. Anyone can make up such a list, and a great many details could be included that do not appear here. It is in the interest of simplicity and brevity that omission is made of all reference to the necessity for the new birth, separation from sin, belief in the Bible as the Word of God, and other prerequisites of such fundamental importance that they must underlie any serious effort to learn the divine plan. Five rules will suffice.

1. There Must Be Honest Willingness to Do God's Will

This may seem so obvious on the face of it, so apparent from what has already been said, that it might be taken for granted, but this seems to be the chief stumbling block for most Christians. As Christ said of the city of Jerusalem which had rejected Him, "Ye would not!" (Matt. 23:37). The human wills of the Jews thwarted His purpose to bless them.

As we are constituted by nature, we prefer our own way. This is the very essence of sin (Isa. 53:6). Self-will keeps more people from enjoying the blessings of the God-planned life than any other factor. They reserve the right to refuse to do what God indicates as His choice for them. They plead with God to be allowed to have what they want, instead of resting in His wisdom and love. Parents who have demanded that a dying child be restored to them have lived to regret bitterly their insistence on their own way. Young people who have married in defiance of the warning against the unequal yoke have paid dearly for self-will.

The prophet Balaam provides us with an illustration. The princes of Moab wanted him to curse Israel. When he asked God about it, the answer was, "Thou shalt not go with him" (Num. 22:12). This was an explicit and plain direction, *the directive will of God.* But Balaam was not satisfied. When greater earthly honor and reward were offered him than before, he went to the Lord once more, hoping that God had changed His mind. The second reply he got is an example of *the permissive will of*

God. With fine irony, God allowed the prophet to have his own way (vv. 20, 22). Balaam went on from disobedience to the express revelation of God's plan for him, to open sin (Num. 31:16), and finally to death by violence, which overtook him in the midst of his anticipated enjoyment of the wages of unrighteousness (Josh. 13:22).

2. God's Will Is Always in Harmony with God's Word

If we feel a desire to do something that conflicts with the plain teaching of the Bible, we may be sure the prompting comes from the world, the flesh, or the devil. It cannot be the will of God, because He cannot contradict Himself. Every opportunity we face, every "leading" we think might be from the Lord, must be tested by the written Word. In this we have the example of Christ when He was tempted by Satan to act of His own volition, apart from the Father's will. He gave us the secret of victory in the words, "It is written" (Luke 4:4, 8).

Certain occupations are at once excluded by the Bible as unfit for Christians. We may not take a position which would require us to bear false witness or to be dishonest. We must avoid any work that would put us in the position of ministering to the weakness or the sin of someone else. The Scriptures seek to guard us against the way of wickedness. "Avoid it, pass not by it, turn from it, and pass away" (Prov. 4:14, 15). Temptation to evil is to be avoided as much as possible (Matt. 6:13).

Where God has already given clear directions about a certain matter, He cannot be expected to make a personal revelation about it to someone who is ignorant of His Word through neglect, or who dislikes the Bible's teaching. Stealing, murder, adultery, covetousness and a host of other sins named in Scripture are always wrong, no matter what the circumstances. God has revealed His will about almost every conceivable problem of human conduct. A passage whose meaning may be obscure to us must never be allowed to make us forget a plain "Thou shalt not."

Some strange errors exist as to how we should use the Bible for our guidance. It is a magic oracle to some people. Instead of feeding regularly on its teachings, they open it at random, look at the first verse that meets their eye, and take it as God's message to them for the moment. There is no doubt that God has often brought a certain verse to the attention of one of His children in an unusual and almost miraculous manner for a special need, but the Word was never intended to be consulted in a superstitious manner.

Others are always "putting out a fleece," yet there is no verse instructing us to do what Gideon did in his hour of weakness, during a terrible national crisis when a greater responsibility rested upon him than most of us are called to bear. The "sign" of Judges 6:17 and the miracles of verses 37-40 were given to a man who had no Bible to teach him, as we have, and at a time when God was pleased to attest His messengers to distinguish them from false prophets.

When Zacharias, in New Testament days, asked for a sign to confirm the word of God's angel, he was stricken dumb because he did not believe (Luke 1:18-20). In view of Christ's words, "An evil and adulterous generation seeketh after a sign" (Matt. 12:39), we must be careful that our "fleece" is not simply an evidence of unbelief or unwillingness to do what we know God wants us to do.

Of course, God in His grace has often honored the faith of those who, having exhausted every other means of knowing His will without apparent success, have asked Him for some indication of what they should do, to keep them from making a serious mistake. But in the experience of great saints of God, such cases are the exception and not the rule.

In cases of doubt, a more reasonable use of the Scriptures is followed by many Christians. They set aside an evening for the reading of the Word, and they read with the earnest prayer that God will speak to their hearts from His Book in their extremity, and suit some part of it to the immediate need.

Thus, one believer, faced with two possible courses to pursue, both equally desirable and in keeping with God's previously revealed plan, began reading in the Psalms, seeking light from the Lord. At length his heart was warmed by one verse which fitted the situation. He made that verse his prayer, believing God had spoken through it in answer to his earlier petitions. It was, "Cause me to hear thy lovingkindness in the morning; for in thee do I trust: cause me to know the way wherein I should walk; for I lift up my soul unto thee" (Ps. 143:8). He was awakened the next day by the ringing of the telephone, and the message was of such a nature that his choice was easy.

3. Providential Circumstances May Indicate God's Will

Where everything in our present circumstances is directly opposed to something we should like to think is the Lord's will for us, we must be careful lest we be insisting on our own way rather than His. He is the God of circumstance. He can, and will, change every factor in a given situation, if He wants us somewhere else than where we are.

Sometimes the romance of the mission field has made young people feel "a call" to go to a far country, but they never were able to go, try as they might. Since it is impossible for God to call someone to do a work for Him without providing for every need and removing every obstacle, the young people simply misunderstood the will of God. "Let every man abide in the same calling wherein he was called" (I Cor. 7:20).

One young man, after an unusual experience at conversion, felt that God wanted him to enter a school in a distant city to study for a certain profession. He was so sure of this that he went. Everything seemed to favor this action, except the circumstances of his home life. It was not long before a verse of Scripture, previously overlooked, made him return home again, to wait upon God for a less hasty "leading." The verse was I Timothy 5:8: "But if any provide not for his own, and specially for those of his own house, he hath denied the faith, and is worse than an infidel."

When the providence of God brought Joseph into Egypt as a slave, he made the best of the situation by faithfully serving God in the work at hand. Moses might have longed to be with his people Israel during the years he was a shepherd in the desert, but he waited until God intervened to bring about a change in his circumstances. It is quite possible that Dorcas would have liked a less obscure place in the early Church than she occupied as a maker of garments (Acts 9:39), but she carried on faithfully for the Lord where she was, and she was raised from the dead to continue her work, while James the apostle was not (Acts 12:2).

It seems clear that providential events must have been linked with the heavenly vision which made Paul and his friends assuredly gather that God wanted them to enter Europe instead of Asia and Bithynia (Acts 16:10). Sometimes the apostle found circumstances demanded that he work at his trade as a tentmaker (Acts 18:3), even though "the Lord ordained that they which preach the gospel should live of the gospel" (I Cor. 9:14). He wrote, "I have learned, in whatsoever state I am, therewith to be content. I know both how to be abased, and I know how to abound: everywhere and in all things I am instructed both to be full and to be hungry, both to abound and to suffer need" (Phil. 4:11, 12).

Our present position is where we must begin to fulfill God's plan. A new environment will not change us into faithful servants of the Lord, if we are not faithful where we are. Christ said, "Ye shall be witnesses unto me both in Jerusalem, and in all Judea, and in Samaria, and unto the uttermost part of the earth" (Acts 1:8). If we do not begin at home, at our Jerusalem, we cannot expect the Lord to enlarge our horizon, nor should we think His will for us will involve a sudden, miraculous change in the circumstances where His providence has already placed us. Let us rest in the Lord where we are, and wait patiently for Him. He will exalt us in due time.

4. God's Will Is Made Known in Answer to Prayer

After the conversion of Paul on the Damascus road, "he trembling and astonished said, Lord, what wilt thou have me to do? And the Lord said unto him, Arise, and go into the city, and it shall be told thee what thou must do" (Acts 9:6). The desire which we find in our own hearts to know God's plan is but a faint reflection of the desire which is in the heart of God. His Word teaches us to pray, "Thou art my rock and my fortress; therefore for thy name's sake lead me, and guide me" (Ps. 31:3); "Make thy way straight before my face" (Ps. 5:8); "Teach me thy way, O Lord; I will walk in thy truth" (Ps. 86:11).

Those who are most often in communion with the Lord are likely to be least often troubled about His will. When we begin the day with a period of early morning devotions, we are made sensitive to His leading during the hours which follow. As we face important decisions, it is easy to lift our hearts to Him for help. We should never step out on ground over which we have not first prayed. God's Word offers us wisdom as we need it (James 1:5). We are liable to make a serious mistake if we seize some opportunity we think is God-given, without earnest prayer.

5. Peace of Mind Should Attend the Doing of God's Will

It is quite evident that the divine program will be in accordance with the convictions of our highest judgment, as illuminated by the Holy Spirit. There should be nothing, ordinarily, to disturb our assurance that we are in God's will. We are promised "the peace of God, which passeth all understanding" (Phil. 4:7). "Great peace have they which love thy law: and nothing shall offend them" (Ps. 119:165). If this is absent, there is something wrong, and we had better go again to the Word of God and to prayer, or re-examine the circumstances.

Every means we have used to learn the mind of the Lord should be in agreement with every other means. He cannot deny Himself, and therefore the teaching of Scripture, the answers to our prayers, the providential position in which we find ourselves, and our own intelligent convictions should all be in harmony.

This consent of the mind to the leading of the Lord, this recognition that His will is good, acceptable and perfect, by which peace concerning the future comes to us, is a ministry of "the spirit of wisdom," who enlightens the eyes of our understanding (Eph. 1:17, 18). It is sometimes called "spiritual intuition," "spiritual intelligence," or an "inner light." Since many evil spirits are in the world whose intent is to deceive the unwary, we must always keep this inner persuasion that we know the will of the Lord in its proper place of subjection to the appointed means of learning His will. "Beloved, believe not every spirit, but try the spirits whether they are of God" (I John

4:1). As we walk close by the Lord, "the anointing which ye have received of him abideth in you, and ye need not that any man teach you" (I John 2:27). As long as we do His blessed will, we shall know of the teaching, whether it be of God (John 7:17).

Probably no better brief statement on how to discover the will of God has ever been written than that by which George Mueller, one of the outstanding Christian leaders of the last century, guided his own life for Christ.

"(1) I seek at the beginning to get my heart into such a state that it has no will of its own in regard to a given matter. Nine-tenths of the trouble with people is just here. Nine-tenths of the difficulties are overcome when our hearts are ready to do the Lord's will, whatever it may be. When one is truly in this state, it is usually but a little way to the knowledge of what His will is.

"(2) Having done this, I do not leave the result to feeling or simple impression. If I do so, I make myself liable to great delusions.

"(3) I see the will of the Spirit of God through, or in connection with the Word of God. The Spirit and the Word must be combined. If I look to the Spirit alone without the Word, I lay myself open to great delusions also. If the Holy Spirit guides us at all, He will do it according to the Scriptures and never contrary to them.

"(4) Next I take into account providential circumstances. These often plainly indicate God's will in connection with His Word and Spirit.

"(5) I ask God in prayer to reveal His will to me aright.

"(6) Thus, through prayer to God, the study of the Word, and reflection, I come to a deliberate judgment according to the best of my ability and knowledge; and if my mind is thus at peace, and continues so after two or three more petitions, I proceed accordingly. In trivial matters, and in transactions involving most important issues, I have found this method always effective."

9

DIFFICULT QUESTIONS

ONE OF THE MOST POPULAR FEATURES of Bible conferences for young people is the question and answer period. The fact that the same practical problems of the Christian life come up for discussion repeatedly, in various parts of the country, is an indication that there is a widespread need for a frank statement about them, in the light of the Scriptures and the available facts.

When young people inquire about matters which puzzle them, they expect a straightforward answer. Which amusements are right for believers? Which ones are wrong, and just why are they wrong? What about friendships with unbelievers? Can a Protestant boy expect happiness if he marries a Catholic girl? Should Christians attend baseball and football games? What is the harm in cards, in smoking, in dancing, in lotteries? How about the movies, the theater, the opera? Is there any reason why a Christian girl should not dress like her schoolmates? Are jazz and swing music all right?

These are typical questions. Those who ask them have every right to a clear and unequivocal answer from their spiritual leaders. Unfortunately, they do not always receive it. There is sometimes a division of opinion among speakers at a conference. Uncertainty and spiritual unrest are the inevitable result. If the leaders disagree, how can young people be expected to discern the truth?

Such disagreements can easily be avoided by keeping personal prejudice out of a discussion, either for or against the point at issue. Whether a given teacher likes or dislikes a particular amusement, whether or not he thinks it right or wrong, should not be made the basis of his answer. There are definite principles of action set forth in the Word of God, and there are facts about most problems which may be ascertained. These are the two elements necessary to a satisfying answer to any question. Personal opinions which ignore the Bible or the facts of the case can bring only confusion. Expressing such opinions is scarcely being fair to the eager minds of young Christians.

Consider the Scripture

The answer to every difficulty ever faced by the human heart is to be found in the Scripture. When a problem is faced honestly, with perfect willingness to obey the Word, there is usually no question about the solution. "If any of you lack wisdom, let him ask of God . . . and it shall be given him" (James 1:5). If we really want to know whether something is pleasing to the Lord, He will not permit us to remain long in the dark about it. Ordinarily, the trouble is not lack of teaching in the Bible so much as unwillingness to follow what it does teach. The key to knowing the mind of Christ is readiness to do His will when it is revealed.

The great principles stated in the New Testament to govern us in doubtful matters are best understood in the light of the early history of the Church. In apostolic days, the Church was faced with problems just as we are today. In the wisdom of God, they were solved in such a way as to provide guideposts for believers during all the changing centuries to follow.

Some problems had to do with matters which were plainly sin. These were dealt with in no uncertain fashion. Believers were forbidden to take each other to court (I Cor. 6:1-8). Those guilty of sins against the body were condemned (I Cor. 5). Obedience to government was enjoined (Rom. 13:1-7). Many such clear commands are to be found.

Ancient Difficulties

There were other problems, however, which did not involve clear-cut moral and ethical issues. They dealt rather with matters of personal choice, where no written law of God applied, now that Christ had become "the end of the law for righteousness to every one that believeth" (Rom. 10:4). Instead of a "thou shalt not" in these cases where godly men might differ, the Holy Spirit was pleased to enunciate principles for the guidance of believers ever afterward. The two difficulties which gave rise to these fundamental rules had to do with the eating of meats which had been offered for sacrifice in idol temples, and with the observing of certain days as holier than others.

In great cities like Rome and Corinth, meat dealers secured their supplies partly from pagan temples where the animals had been offered in sacrifice. One could not always tell whether a purchase came from this source or from another. Nor did anyone care very much until the gospel came and Christians began to face the question of how they should conduct themselves in pagan surroundings.

Should believers use meat which might have come from an idol temple? There was a division of opinion. One group refused to eat meat of any kind. Even though it might not have been dedicated to some pagan god, it was likely to be ceremonially unclean as judged by the law of Moses. The other group held that it was perfectly proper for them to eat what they pleased. A pagan ceremony could not affect the essential qualities of the food they found offered for sale, and is not every creature of God good (I Tim. 4:3-5)?

The second subject of controversy was concerned with the keeping of special days. Christians with a Jewish background liked to observe the holy days of ancient Israel. The Jewish Sabbath was a convenient time for worship. Others preferred to follow the example of the apostles by meeting on the Lord's Day (Luke 24:33-36; Acts 20:7). Still others regarded every day as holy unto the Lord (Rom. 14:5), and they tried to make every day the same in the life they lived for Him.

Guiding Principles

Both of these problems were dealt with in such a way as to make it possible for the Church to solve every point of dispute in the future. Instead of treating the two questions as temporary difficulties which would lose their significance with the passing of time, the Holy Spirit devoted three long passages of the New Testament to them, making them the basis of principles to be followed throughout the entire Church Age. The extended discussion of these sample problems is found in Romans 14; I Corinthians 8; 10:23-33.

First of all, the proper attitude of Christians toward those who differed with them was enunciated in Romans 14:1-4. The man who restricted his diet to vegetables was forbidden to sit in judgment on his brother who ate whatever he wanted. On the other hand, the man who was convinced that there was no wrong in eating doubtful meats was told not to despise his brother who refused them.

The bearing of this passage of Scripture on young people's problems today is of great importance. No one has the right to stand on a platform and say, "You are sinning if you do the thing I consider wrong," when the Bible has not ruled on the matter. Neither has anyone the right to accuse someone else of narrowness or bigotry because that person conscientiously refrains from something in which others see no harm. Nor is there justification here for thinking ourselves to be strong in the faith just because we have no compunctions about indulging in a questionable pleasure, for it may contain elements which mark it as contrary to the spirit of Christ.

To abstain from fleshly lusts requires a stronger faith than to indulge them. A Christian who remains aloof from a doubtful practice just because he wants to please Christ is giving evidence of spiritual health quite beyond that of the self-indulgent man who has never given up anything for the Lord's sake.

FIRST PRINCIPLE: *Personal Liberty in Christ*

There is abundant testimony in the Bible to the fact that we have freedom of action as children of God, within the limits He has set. The law as a "yoke of bondage" has been lifted from us (Gal. 5:1). Once Israel was given laws about meats. Now, "meat commendeth us not to God: for neither, if we eat, are we the better; neither, if we eat not, are we the worse" (I Cor. 8:8).

Once there were laws given about holy days. Now, "one man esteemeth one day above another: another esteemeth every day alike. Let every man be fully persuaded in his own mind" (Rom. 14:5). It is quite evident that God has placed Christian conduct on a different basis from that of Israel, in cases where there is no moral issue involved. We now have freedom to serve the Lord in accordance with the dictates of our own conscience, subject only to His Word and His Spirit (Gal. 5:16, 18).

This first principle lifts the spirit of bondage from the believer (Rom. 8:15). Considered apart from other higher principles of action, it helps to solve some problems which have perplexed Christians, such as the Sunday question. There are young people whose only means of livelihood involves work on Sunday, because they are connected, let us say, with an industry which provides light, heat, water or transportation to an entire community, with its churches and hospitals. Are they sinning against God, and are others sinning who use the public services which make Sunday employment necessary? The principle of Christian liberty makes it clear that this is not at all a question of breaking the law of God, and the burden is gone from many a conscience.

We gather for worship on Sunday by common consent, and not because the law of the Lord requires that particular day. God has always honored such gatherings, ever since the Lord Jesus was present at the first one (Luke 24:36), but He has also honored the testimony of individuals who were unable to be present for reasons they could conscientiously give to Him. There is a basic human need for which God made provision by giving Israel the Sabbath at Sinai (Neh. 9:13, 14). We will do all we can to keep the Lord's Day holy unto Him, out of love for Him, but we know that He understands if we must work on that day. "Let no man therefore judge you . . . in respect of an holy day . . . or of the sabbath days" (Col. 2:16).

Likewise, we are not sinning against the law of Christ if we partake of foods once forbidden Israel. There are important sanitary reasons, since discovered by science, why God did not permit His people to eat the flesh of scavengers, carnivorous animals and other "unclean beasts." It is profitable to know the ancient regulations governing clean and unclean animals, but the Christian who eats ham, for example, is not a lawbreaker. "There is nothing unclean of itself: but to him that esteemeth anything to be unclean, to him it is unclean" (Rom. 14:14).

There are definite limits to the first principle of action set forth in the Word. The liberty wherewith Christ has made us free is not liberty to sin. "Shall we sin, because we are not under the law, but under grace? God forbid" (Rom 6:15). Those who practice sin have simply never been born again. "Whosoever is born of God doth not practice sin" (I John 3:9, marg.). Repeatedly, the Holy Spirit warns us against misunderstanding or twisting the blessed teaching about liberty in Christ, in such a way as to result in harm. "Brethren, ye have been called unto liberty; only use not liberty for an occasion to the flesh, but by love serve one another" (Gal. 5:13). We are free so that we may voluntarily become servants of Christ (I Cor. 7:22).

Every scripture dealing with our own spiritual progress may be said to limit the principle of liberty in Christ. We are not free to neglect the Bible, prayer, Christian witness, the fellowship of other Christians, our responsibilities to the church, to our fellow men, or to God. We are not free to do anything which tends to injure our bodies, which are the temples of the Holy Spirit (I Cor. 6:19, 20). We are to "seek those things which are above, where Christ sitteth on the right hand of God" (Col. 3:1), to walk worthy of the calling wherewith we are called (Eph. 4:1), and to be faithful in everything that is part of our duty and privilege as believers.

SECOND PRINCIPLE: *Our Neighbor's Good*

This is a higher motive for action than personal liberty. "All things are lawful; but not all things are expedient.

All things are lawful; but not all things edify. Let no man seek his own, but each his neighbor's good" (I Cor. 10:23, 24, A.S.V.). That which might be perfectly all right for us, if we judged it by its effect on our own spiritual lives, might be very wrong when judged by its effect on a weaker Christian. "Take heed lest by any means this liberty of yours become a stumbling block to them that are weak" (I Cor. 8:9).

Here is a man, let us say, who likes to see horses running. It is lawful for him to do so. If he attended a horse race, his own spiritual life might not be harmed. But he has a friend or neighbor who has a weakness for gambling. This friend is led by his example to go to the races. The effect of the crowd of ungodly folk placing their wagers is strong enough to awaken in this second man a passion to win a little easy money, as some of them seem to be doing. He is soon plunged into soul-destroying sin, which ruins not only himself but his family. The Christian responsible has paid a terrible price for pleasing himself.

A more common illustration is to be seen in the Christian who "takes a drink." Medical science has discovered that a certain percentage of all drinkers become drunkards. No one can tell which man or woman has this unsuspected weakness. Through the influence of a man who is able to drink with moderation, another man is led to take his first glass of liquor. This second individual finds that a sleeping demon has been awakened. He becomes an alcoholic, a pitiable slave to his addiction.

"Destroy not him with thy meat, for whom Christ died" (Rom 14:15). We may put any questionable amusement or habit or practice in the place of the word "meat," in this or the parallel verses stating the same great principle. When others are hurt by our self-indulgence, we are not walking in love. When we embolden the conscience of a weak brother by something we do which does not seem to hurt us, so that he is ruined, we sin against our brother, and therefore we sin against Christ, even though no law has been written about that particular matter of indulgence (I Cor. 8:10-12).

A great many young people's problems would be solved if this rule were universally adopted. Anything is wrong which might lead someone else astray. If it could keep an unsaved person from seriously considering the salvation we profess, then let us avoid it for their sakes, no matter how harmless it might otherwise be.

The apostle Paul by inspiration stated this principle emphatically as his own rule of life, in writing to the churches of Corinth and Rome. "Wherefore, if meat make my brother to offend, I will eat no flesh while the world standeth, lest I make my brother to offend" (I Cor. 8:13). "It is good neither to eat flesh, nor to drink wine, nor anything whereby thy brother stumbleth, or is offended, or is made weak" (Rom. 14:21).

It was because of this principle that the Lord Jesus performed the miracle of the tribute money. He, the Creator and Sustainer of the universe, might have been considered above the necessity of paying taxes to the Roman government, but He sent Peter for the money and gave as the reason, "lest we should offend them" (Matt. 17:27). We too must "provide things honest in the sight of all men" (Rom. 12:17). We are required to "abstain from all appearance of evil" (I Thess. 5:22).

THIRD PRINCIPLE: *The Glory of God*

"Whether therefore ye eat, or drink, or whatsoever ye do, do all to the glory of God" (I Cor. 10:31). This is the highest motive one can possibly follow: to do everything so that honor and praise may accrue to God. How we may seek to conform our actions to this ideal is suggested in a related series of exhortations in Colossians 3:17, 23: "And whatsoever ye do in word or deed, do all in the name of the Lord Jesus, giving thanks to God and the Father by him . . . And whatsoever ye do, do it heartily, as to the Lord, and not unto men."

Here are three distinct tests which may be applied to a given act:

(1) Can it be done in the name of the Lord Jesus? That is, can we do it as those who bear His name before others, bringing praise and honor to His name instead of reproach?

(2) Can we perform the action thankfully, expressing gratitude to God for the privilege, and asking His blessing upon it in prayer?

(3) Is it possible for us to do it heartily as unto the Lord, which means for His sake, and as though He were present?

This principle applies to actions which could have little or no effect on our neighbors. For example, we are free to use our spare time as we please, within certain limits. We find ourselves alone. Shall we read a questionable magazine, or a profitable book? Shall we play solitaire, or study the Scriptures? Shall we do our home work, or listen to the radio? If we have in view the glory of God, it will make a difference in our choice. What will be most likely to produce in us that which will enable us better to represent Him as His ambassadors? If we are weary, either rest or relaxation is doubtless the answer. If our work at school is a discredit to the Lord we love, we had better study. If we have been too much indoors, a walk or a bicycle ride may be the best thing we could do for God's glory.

Let us apply this third principle to the subject of sports. It is evident that we have personal liberty to engage in any beneficial recreation. Likewise, there is no honest basis for refusing to play a clean game, or to watch such a game, lest some weak brother be led astray. What about the third rule for action? Can we play tennis or baseball, or shoot at a target, to the glory of God? Most certainly we can!

The Lord knows our frame. He has made us so that physical and mental exercises are necessary to our wellbeing, when indulged temperately. All work and no play makes Jack a dull boy. If our recreation is such that it can be enjoyed without bringing any discredit on the name of the Lord, with thanksgiving for the privilege, and heartily as unto Him, we may be sure we are doing no wrong to enter wholeheartedly into the fun. On the other hand, if it is something we would not want to do if He were present, because we know it might harm us morally, physically or spiritually, we had better leave it alone.

Let us suppose that a game becomes an obsession. We would rather play basketball than eat. It begins to result in the neglect of other things. Our grades at school are not good. We no longer find time for Bible study and Christian fellowship and service. Or perhaps we are spending more money than we should on football games. Or we have taken up something which begins to injure our health, or threatens to keep us from giving an honest day's work for an honest day's pay.

What then? We still have liberty in Christ. We still may feel that we are not a stumbling block before others; our influence is not hurting anyone else. But anything which adversely affects our spiritual life, undermines our health, or tends to hurt our testimony before the world is not something that can be said to glorify God. We love Him; we are sincere in our desire to serve the One who has saved us. Therefore, we must restore the balance to our lives by putting recreation back where it belongs. We must put first things first and, even though it might seem like a great sacrifice, give up anything which interferes with our accomplishing the high purpose for which the Lord has placed us on the earth, "that we should be to the praise of his glory" (Eph. 1:12).

10

OPPORTUNITIES FOR TRIUMPH

EVEN AFTER THE GREAT BIBLE PRINCIPLES of Christian conduct have been stated during a discussion, some young people are not sure just what course to pursue in certain matters. In such cases, an intelligent examination of available facts will usually remove any doubt as to the attitude most likely to please the Lord.

It is well to remember that if a thing is questionable, it is probably wrong. If the cleanliness of a white collar or a dress is doubtful, it is dirty. If there is any uncertainty as to the purity of water in a stream, sensible people do not drink it. We do not board a train unless we know where it will take us.

Why should not this customary clear thinking be carried over into the spiritual realm? It is because the flesh has power to blind our eyes to what is good for the soul. We find it easier to take care of our physical health, by rejecting a doubtful lobster salad or refusing to sit in a cold room, than to consider our spiritual health by rejecting a doubtful amusement or refusing to sit in an atmosphere uncongenial to the Christian life. "The lust of the flesh, and the lust of the eyes, and the pride of life" are present to keep us from seeing clearly what is best for us as servants of Christ (I John 2:16).

Spiritual Pride

Before we take up some of the specific problems which
appear again and again at meetings of young people, it is
well to recall that there are other problems, seldom mentioned, which are much more serious. Some Christians
are inclined to make a shibboleth of several pet dislikes
in the matter of "questionable amusements," and
assume an attitude which says, if you do these things you
are not faithful to Christ. In their own opinion, they are
on a higher spiritual plane simply because of what they
do not do. Such persons might be shocked if it were
suggested that Luke 18:9-14 had some application to
them.

Christ spoke a parable "unto certain which trusted in
themselves that they are righteous, and despised others."
There was a Pharisee who thanked God that he was not
as other men were. He prided himself that he was better
than a poor taxgatherer, who stood some distance away,
crying out to God as a needy sinner. Christ's illuminating
comment was that the sinner, aware of his sins, was ac-
cepted with God rather than the man who congratulated
himself on his goodness.

There are men who do not gamble at cards, but who
treat their wives with carelessness and selfishness. Yet
the Scripture says, "Husbands, love your wives" (Eph.
5:25). There are women who are models of sweetness in
public, but who disobey Ephesians 5:22 and I Peter 3:1-6
by shrewish actions at home, nagging their husbands and
screaming at their children. There are others who neglect
their families in total disregard of Titus 2:4, 5.

Evil Speaking

Young people have been driven away from churches,
where they might have become Christian leaders, by the
evil tongues of persons who condemned them for some

practice, not wicked in itself, nor condemned in the Bible, but which had been made a pet criterion of spiritual health. It is still true that tongues may be "set on fire of hell" (James 3:6). It is possible to abstain from pleasures considered doubtful, while being guilty of sins plainly named in the Word.

Sometimes the spectacle is seen of a faithful church officer, a man of integrity and a winner of souls, severely criticized because of a fleshly habit he has not been able to overcome, while those who attack him are injuring the work of God far more seriously by their bitterness, malice and talebearing. They suppose they have a high standing in heaven because they have not his weakness; he smites his breast and cries out to the Lord over his human frailties, and finds God honoring his testimony.

Augustine, a famous saint of God, born in A.D. 353, gave to the Church a proverbial saying worth remembering: "In essentials, unity; in nonessentials, liberty; in all things, charity." Where the Bible has ruled on a subject there can be no honest difference of opinion. But where the Bible has not ruled, we must ask ourselves, "Who art thou that judgest another man's servant? to his own master he standeth or falleth. Yea, he shall be holden up: for God is able to make him stand" (Rom. 14:4).

As we consider some of the things found on most lists of "thou shalt not's," let us be crystal clear in our thinking about this whole matter. Who is it that holds a certain pleasure to be wrong? If it is our parents, we owe them our honor and respect. If it is our pastor, he is watching over our souls, as one who must give account (Heb. 13:17). If it is our own conscience, we must take heed lest we defile it (I Cor. 8:7). If it is the view of our own church or denomination, it certainly deserves a hearing, for it seeks to protect us.

The individual who thinks he is a "separated Christian" solely because he subscribes to a man-made list of tests for consecrated character is likely to have some unhappy experiences awaiting him, no matter who made up the list of taboos. We need what a great man of God in another century called "the expulsive power of a new affection." Love for the Saviour who died for us is the only power which can enable us to win our struggle against self-indulgence and sin. We can do through Him what we never could do in our own strength.

No course of study could anticipate every difficulty which may come in the next generation, or treat of every current doubtful matter to the perfect satisfaction of everyone. There are undoubtedly outstanding Christians who live and deport themselves in a manner not considered quite proper by other outstanding Christians with a different background and environment. Yet there are also some who make an issue of these outward taboos, who nevertheless are guilty of spiritual sins listed by name in the Scriptures as among the most serious and harmful which could be committed.

It does not become any of us to set ourselves up as judges of our brethren in the Lord. Self-judgment is plainly enjoined in I Corinthians 11:31, but the judging of others is as plainly forbidden in Matthew 7:1 and Romans 14:4. Let us in every matter of difficulty apply the principles set forth in the Word for our guidance. Let us be strict with ourselves, careful about our testimony to neighbors, jealous for the glory and honor of the Lord Jesus, but charitable in our attitude toward our brethren whom Christ has received.